THE IMPACT OF THE 2008 OLYMPIC GAMES ON HUMAN RIGHTS AND THE RULE OF LAW IN CHINA

HEARING

BEFORE THE

CONGRESSIONAL-EXECUTIVE COMMISSION ON CHINA

ONE HUNDRED TENTH CONGRESS

SECOND SESSION

FEBRUARY 27, 2008

Printed for the use of the Congressional-Executive Commission on China

Available via the World Wide Web: http://www.cecc.gov

U.S. GOVERNMENT PRINTING OFFICE

41–150 PDF   WASHINGTON : 2008

For sale by the Superintendent of Documents, U.S. Government Printing Office
Internet: bookstore.gpo.gov   Phone: toll free (866) 512–1800; DC area (202) 512–1800
Fax: (202) 512–2104   Mail: Stop IDCC, Washington, DC 20402–0001

CONGRESSIONAL-EXECUTIVE COMMISSION ON CHINA

LEGISLATIVE BRANCH COMMISSIONERS

House

SANDER LEVIN, Michigan, *Chairman*
MARCY KAPTUR, Ohio
MICHAEL M. HONDA, California
TOM UDALL, New Mexico
TIMOTHY J. WALZ, Minnesota
DONALD A. MANZULLO, Illinois
JOSEPH R. PITTS, Pennsylvania
EDWARD R. ROYCE, California
CHRISTOPHER H. SMITH, New Jersey

Senate

BYRON DORGAN, North Dakota, *Co-Chairman*
MAX BAUCUS, Montana
CARL LEVIN, Michigan
DIANNE FEINSTEIN, California
SHERROD BROWN, Ohio
SAM BROWNBACK, Kansas
CHUCK HAGEL, Nebraska
GORDON H. SMITH, Oregon
MEL MARTINEZ, Florida

EXECUTIVE BRANCH COMMISSIONERS

PAULA DOBRIANSKY, Department of State
CHRISTOPHER R. HILL, Department of State
HOWARD M. RADZELY, Department Labor

DOUGLAS GROB, *Staff Director*
CHARLOTTE OLDHAM-MOORE, *Deputy Staff Director*

(II)

CONTENTS

IV

THE IMPACT OF THE 2008 OLYMPIC GAMES ON HUMAN RIGHTS AND THE RULE OF LAW IN CHINA

WEDNESDAY, FEBRUARY 27, 2008

CONGRESSIONAL-EXECUTIVE
COMMISSION ON CHINA,
Washington, DC.

The hearing was convened, pursuant to notice, at 2:30 p.m., in room B-318, Rayburn House Office Building, Representative Sander Levin (Chairman of the Commission) presiding.

Also present: Senator Byron Dorgan, Co-Chairman; Senator Mel Martinez; Representative Joseph R. Pitts; Representative Tim Walz; Representative Edward R. Royce; Representative Michael M. Honda; Representative Christopher H. Smith; Representative Donald A. Manzullo; and Representative Marcy Kaptur.

OPENING STATEMENT OF HON. SANDER LEVIN, A U.S. REPRESENTATIVE FROM MICHIGAN, CHAIRMAN, CONGRESSIONAL-EXECUTIVE COMMISSION ON CHINA

Chairman LEVIN. Well, let's begin. We'll do so with opening statements. There is going to be a House vote in 15 or 20 minutes, and Senator Dorgan and the other Commissioners will carry on. We'll try to miss as little of the testimony as possible.

All of you were excellent in submitting your testimony in advance, and somewhat well in advance, which is not always true, so we have all had a chance to read your testimony. Your testimony will be entered into the record. As Senator Dorgan and I will indicate, you can do whatever you want with your five minutes, either going over it in its entirety if you can do so in five minutes, or summarizing, hitting high points, whatever you would like to do. We very much look forward to this hearing and thank all of you for coming.

Indeed, this hearing embodies why this commission was created some years ago. The Commission convenes this hearing to examine the likely impact of the 2008 Summer Olympics on human rights and the rule of law in China. In its Olympic bid documents and its preparations for the 2008 Summer Games, China made commitments pertaining to human rights and the rule of law. Our witnesses today will help us to evaluate those commitments and to assess the openness with which China has allowed the rest of the world to monitor its progress in fulfilling them.

In the days before the International Olympic Committee voted to select Beijing, there was consideration of human rights and related

(1)

issues, as had been the case—and I emphasize this—in previous deliberations about appropriate sites for the Olympics. China made a point of raising the link between human rights and the 2008 Games. On July 12, 2001, the state-run China Daily reported that Wang Wei, the Secretary General of the Beijing Olympics Bid Committee, said, "We are confident that the Games coming to China not only promotes our economy, but also enhances all social conditions, including education, health, and human rights." These words could not have been clearer. Human rights in the 2008 Olympics were linked before Beijing was awarded the Games, and China itself linked them.

Just yesterday, China's Foreign Minister announced that China is ready to resume the human rights dialogue with the United States that was suspended in 2004. That announcement underlines the relevance of this hearing—which was announced several weeks ago—and means that there is considerable and appropriate ground to cover today.

On press freedom, Beijing's bid documents state, "There will be no restrictions on journalists and reporting of the Olympic Games." At the same time they also stated, "There will be no restriction concerning the use of media material produced in China and intended primarily for broadcast outside."

On openness in general, Beijing's action plan for the Olympics states, "In the preparation for the Games we will be open in every aspect to the rest of the country and the whole world."

On government transparency, more specifically, Beijing's action plan for the Olympics states, "Government work will be open to public supervision and information concerning major Olympic construction projects shall be made available regularly."

This last point deserves extra attention because it underscores the importance of China's new regulation on the public disclosure of government information which takes effect on May 1 of this year. This new regulation promises people in China the legal means to obtain access to government records relating to construction, labor affairs, health and safety, the environment, and much more before the Games begin, and also after.

Much of the world's attention also has focused on China's environment. Beijing's bid documents stated, "By 2008, the environmental quality in Beijing will be comparable to that of major cities in developed countries, with clean and fresh air, a beautiful environment, and healthy ecology. Meteorological observations in the area of Beijing in the past 10 years have indicated that July and August are good times to hold the Olympic Games."

I must note that China's security preparations for the Olympics also have raised concerns. Congress banned the transfer of crime control equipment to China after the Tiananmen killings of 1989. Nonetheless, recent press reports describe the export from the United States to China of equipment identified as commercial, but with crime control applications.

This merits attention because after the Olympics high-tech surveillance products will be left in the hands of China's public security and state security organs who could use them to monitor political activists, religious practitioners, and members of certain ethnic minority groups.

The Commission asked the Under Secretary of Commerce for Industry and Security, Mario Mancuso, to testify today, but he's in India on official business and unfortunately could not join us. However, he has offered to respond to questions in writing, and we will be submitting them.

So, finally, let me say this. China does not want to be labeled as a gross violator of human rights, and yet it makes its determination to eliminate dissent painfully clear to the world. Thousands of prisoners of conscience languish in jails across China. Just in the last few weeks, China has detained individuals who have mentioned the Olympics when speaking out for human rights. Officials have cast their public-mindedness as a subversion of state power.

These same authorities assert that raising concern over human rights in the context of the 2008 Games violates the Olympic spirit. Nothing could be further from the truth. Fairness on the field of play, fair judgments, and the opportunity to witness human potential unleashed to the fullest extent are the very essence of the Olympic spirit. They are also the essence of freedom and fundamental human rights.

In seeking the 2008 Olympics, China made specific commitments. Seven years have passed, and the Games begin in less than six months. This hearing is a necessary part of determining whether China is fulfilling its commitments. China is, as we all know, an increasingly important part of the international community and it is vital that there be continuing assessment of its commitments, whether as a member of the WTO or as the awarded host of the Olympics. Other nations, including our own, have both the responsibility and a legitimate interest in ensuring compliance with those commitments.

Senator Dorgan, now it is your turn. This is an opportunity for all of us to gather, and it is my pleasure that we can be doing this together.

[The questions to Mr. Mancuso and his responses appear in the appendix.]

[The prepared statement of Chairman Levin appears in the appendix.]

STATEMENT OF HON. BYRON DORGAN, A U.S. SENATOR FROM NORTH DAKOTA, CO-CHAIRMAN, CONGRESSIONAL-EXECUTIVE COMMISSION ON CHINA

Co-Chairman DORGAN. Well, Congressman Levin, thank you very much. I appreciate working with you as co-chair of this important commission.

Let me say that the purpose of this hearing is to evaluate whether the 2008 Olympics will in fact bring benefits, or any lasting benefits, to the Chinese people by enhancing human rights and accelerating rule of law development.

China views the 2008 Olympics as not merely just an athletic event, but as recognition of its global, economic, diplomatic, and military power. It is a way of extending themselves to the world. It is, to them, a political event in many ways, and one of great significance. It will confirm their acceptance in China as a proud and prominent participant on the international stage.

So, now how did China get to this position? China lost its bid in 2000 to host the Olympics and I think in part because of the long shadow cast by the government's crackdown in Tiananmen Square.

The government negotiators for China worked a long time to secure a better outcome on their second effort to host the Olympics, and they were successful, in part, by promising international Olympic Committee members and others that China would commit itself to significant reforms that included international reporters having the unfettered ability to interview, to exercise free speech, and to report. China also responded to the issue of the environment. There is so much that the Chinese promised. Now the question for this hearing is, to what effect, what should we, members of the international community, expect?

Now, there was a hearing before the European Parliament, and I believe I am told that Ms. Hom was a part of that hearing. At that hearing a few months ago, there was a witness named Hu Jia. He called in by telephone to that hearing before the European Parliament. He, as a courageous dissident, addressed the issue of the Olympics and the Chinese Government at the hearing. Well, the hearing was very similar to this one, as I understand it, with witnesses, and then a telephone presentation by Mr. Hu.

One result of that hearing testimony was Mr. Hu being dragged from his house by Chinese state police agents. He now sits in jail. His wife and his three-month-old child are under house arrest in their Beijing apartment. The Chinese Government has a three-month-old under house arrest, mind you, and Mr. Hu sits in jail. Their apartment's telephone and Internet connections are cut. All this, for speaking to a committee—before the European Parliament—very much like this commission. So much for free speech and free expression.

Just last week, Yang Chunlin, an unemployed factory worker, went on trial for subversion in northeast China. He was arrested last year for reportedly helping nearby villagers seek compensation for lost land. He had collected 10,000 signatures from local farmers. The signatures were for a letter that read in part: "We Want Human Rights, Not the Olympics." Prosecutors said that that letter stained China's international image, and that it amounted to subversion, so this unemployed factory worker went on trial.

Mr. Chairman, I am going to ask that we include a list of political prisoners in China, which I have attached to my statement, to be a part of this hearing record. It is a short list; not exhaustive, just representative. A short representative list of those who now sit in prison for the very thing that we will exercise in this room: speaking freely.

We were promised, all of us were promised, the world was promised by the Chinese Government that they would move in the direction of allowing more discussion, free speech, and other freedoms. We are now discovering that that was just a promise. We expect, I hope through this hearing, to hear more about whether and how China is meeting its commitments.

I hope the Chinese Government is listening. I hope they will hear the message from this commission that we expect progress. We expect the Chinese Government to keep its word. We expect the Chinese Government to stop detaining under house arrest three-month-old children. We expect them to release people like Mr. Hu and others from their prisons, people who are jailed precisely because, and only because, they had the courage to speak out and exercise the right of free speech, something we take for granted every single day of our lives here in this great country.

So, Mr. Chairman, I will ask consent that we include in the record this list of political prisoners that I have included in my statement.

Chairman LEVIN. Without any objection, so ordered.

Would anybody else like to make a short statement?

Co-Chairman DORGAN. Mr. Chairman, let me also ask that Senator Hagel's statement be included in the record, at his request.

Chairman LEVIN. Without objection.

So this doesn't always happen at committee or commission meetings. It's usually just two of us. So, let each of us who would like make a short statement, then we'll hear from the witnesses.

[The prepared statement of Co-Chairman Dorgan appears in the appendix.]

[The list of prisoners appears in the appendix.]

[The prepared statement of Senator Hagel appears in the appendix.]

Senator MARTINEZ. Thank you. Let me just say from my standpoint, I just associate myself with the comments of Senator Dorgan and thank the Chair for holding this hearing.

Chairman LEVIN. Thank you very much, Senator. Representative Pitts? Thank you.

STATEMENT OF HON. JOSEPH R. PITTS, A U.S. REPRESENTATIVE FROM PENNSYLVANIA, MEMBER, CONGRESSIONAL-EXECUTIVE COMMISSION ON CHINA

Representative PITTS. Mr. Chairman, thank you for holding this important hearing on "The Impact of the 2008 Olympic Games on Human Rights and the Rule of Law in China." In preparing for this hearing, I have been pleased to see some of the positive changes occurring in China as a result of the government's commitment to uphold the mandate of the Olympic Charter; however, I remain concerned about the staying power of any of these changes. The question remains as to whether or not the people of China will benefit from the increased observation of and attention to Chinese Government regulations on issues as varied as refugees, migrant workers, and the peaceful expression of religious faith.

Over the years, as I have watched changes in China, I have been encouraged and discouraged during countless cycles of two steps forward and then three steps backward. While some might dispute that assessment, the fact that we continue to receive numerous reports about Chinese officials' actions against North Korean refugees, Uighur Muslims in Xinjiang province, child laborers, and Protestant house church leaders and congregants reflects that there still is a long way to go. Unfortunately, the government does not seem bent on protecting, assisting, or improving the lives and/or the peaceful expression of beliefs by any of these groups.

While this hearing focuses on the impact domestically of the Olympics being held in China, there is another side to China's recent and even long-term activities. China's support for the government of Sudan is highly problematic, particularly in light of the rape, death, and destruction occurring in Darfur.

While the Chinese Government making a recent statement to the government of Sudan on this issue is a small positive step, much more pressure and leadership on behalf of the people of Darfur should come from Chinese officials.

Chinese officials constantly use the refrain that they do not interfere in the internal matters of other countries—that is an interesting statement in light of the fact that their presence, money, and resources automatically do interfere in the internal matters of other nations. In Burma, for instance, reports suggest that since 1989, the Chinese Government has provided the dictators in Burma with over 2 billion dollars' worth of weapons and military equipment. This Chinese weaponry has allowed the regime to quadruple the size of its forces to 450,000. As a result, Chinese weaponry has directly contributed to the brutal dictatorship's targeting of children, women, and ethnic groups in its attacks against its population. Chinese officials can't tell me that they have no responsibility for what is going on in Burma—it's simply not true. As is well known, the Burmese regime uses rape as a weapon of terror, uses individuals captured in raids as human landmine sweepers, and destroys food sources, homes, and places of worship. Specifically, the dictators of Burma could not implement their attacks without Chinese weaponry.

In terms of North Korea, the Chinese Government targets North Korean refugees who have fled to China and sends them back to certain torture and likely death at the hands of the North Korean officials. If the Chinese Government refused to deport North Korean refugees and instead allowed, as they should under their international commitments, the UN High Commissioner for Refugees [UNHCR] to assist and resettle the refugees, it would undermine the North Korean Government. China's actions against refugees directly helps the brutal North Korean regime.

The Chinese Government must understand that statements that it does not interfere in the internal affairs of other nations is belied by its actions. If the Chinese Government wants to curtail criticism of its actions, then it needs to implement long-term, lasting changes that improve the lives and protect the freedoms of the Chinese people and other peoples around the world.

I sincerely hope that China's hosting of the Olympics is the first step toward an era of new openness and positive change that will benefit the Chinese people and others. However, only time will tell. I stand with those Chinese journalists, peaceful religious leaders, peaceful political activists, and NGO leaders who continue, with great courage, to fight for change in China.

I look forward to hearing from our very distinguished witnesses and receiving their insights and recommendations on steps the U.S. Government should take to further support the people of China.

Chairman LEVIN. Thank you.

Representative Smith? And let me just mention, I think we are going to have a vote soon. So if each of you could try to summarize, your entire statement will be placed in the record. Chris?

STATEMENT OF HON. CHRISTOPHER H. SMITH, A U.S. REPRESENTATIVE FROM NEW JERSEY, MEMBER, CONGRESSIONAL-EXECUTIVE COMMISSION ON CHINA

Representative SMITH of New Jersey. Thank you very much, Mr. Chairman. Let me just say at the outset that I also serve as Ranking Member on the Africa and Global Health Subcommittee and we have a very important hearing on tuberculosis, so I will have to return to that hearing. As the Ranking Republican, I want to thank our witnesses in advance for the work they are doing here. Like Mr. Pitts and all of our colleagues, all of us have been joined at the hip with Mr. Levin in trying to promote human rights and the rule of law in China.

A few weeks ago, the New York Times reported the arrest of a 34-year-old Chinese dissident named Hu Jia. Mr. Hu's crime? Using his home computer to disseminate information on human rights violations. He joins a huge, ever-growing number of cyber dissidents who today in China are being hauled off to jail simply for promoting human rights and democracy.

The Times article suggests the obvious in the run-up to the Beijing Olympics in August. The People's Republic of China [PRC] is using its iron fist to eradicate dissent. Even Mr. Hu's wife and two-month-old daughter, who are now under house arrest, prompted the Times to note that the baby is probably the youngest political prisoner in China.

But in this particular case we can, and must, take direct action. I'm afraid that many American companies like Google, Microsoft, and Yahoo! have cooperated with the Chinese Government in turning the Internet into a tool of surveillance and censorship. Last year, as some of you may know, I introduced the Global Online Freedom Act, which is making its way through Congress to prevent U.S. high-tech Internet companies from turning information over to the Chinese police that identifies individual Internet users and requires them to disclose how the Chinese version of their search engines censors the Internet. In October, the Foreign Affairs Committee approved it and we hope it will be on the floor soon.

In China—and I think this is the one issue that is often not focused upon—the whole issue of the one-child-per-couple policy continues to be one of the most egregious human rights violations, especially against women and especially against children, ever perpetuated in human kind.

The one-child-per-couple policy, with its heavy reliance on forced abortion and coerced sterilization, has led to an unbelievable, disproportionate number of girl children and girl babies. One estimate puts it at as many as 100 million missing girls in China as directly attributable to more than 30 years of one-child-per-couple, which went into effect in 1979. This is gendercide. These children, these girls, are targeted simply because they are little girls. My wife and I have four children. If we lived in China, we would have one, maybe Melissa. The other three would be dead, because brothers and sisters are illegal in that particular country.

We also know that there is no religious freedom, that the house church movement continues to be suppressed, the Falun Gong, the Uighurs. I do believe the Olympics give us a window of opportunity that we can ill afford not to seize to raise these issues robustly, and hopefully have an impact. That is why this hearing is being held.

Finally, the Chinese Government needs to crack down and we need to investigate this whole issue of bodies. I know you are all following it; "20/20," Harry Wu, and so many others have raised the issue, as it ought to be raised: how did those individuals get the plasticization that has occurred to their bodies, many of these men and women, very much in the prime of their life?

I happen to believe, having actually been in a Laogai prison camp soon after Tiananmen Square, Prison Camp #1 in Beijing, that they have been shot. We were looking for more evidence, but all of the evidence suggests—but has not yet been proven—that they are there through a very nefarious way and we need to investigate that as well.

Again, Mr. Chairman, my full statement will be made a part of the record. But human rights in China are non-existent—and I would just add this. The United Nations needs to step up to the plate. The Human Rights Council has not done its work. China is a member in good standing, and when that went from the Human Rights Commission to the Human Rights Council, all of these promises were made about how that new body would represent an honest, transparent, aggressive, and incisive look, particularly at countries that are part of the council. Nothing could be further from the truth. Other treaty bodies, genocide conventions, conventions against torture, all those others need to step up to the plate because they have not done the kind of scrutiny on China that they need to do.

Thank you, Mr. Chairman.

[The prepared statement of Representative Smith appears in the appendix.]

Chairman LEVIN. Thank you.

Senator Dorgan and I have quietly consulted. If each of the rest of you could take just a minute, try to do that so that we can get to the witnesses.

Representative Walz?

STATEMENT OF HON. TIM WALZ, A U.S. REPRESENTATIVE FROM MINNESOTA, MEMBER, CONGRESSIONAL-EXECUTIVE COMMISSION ON CHINA

Representative WALZ. Thank you, Mr. Chairman and our colleague from the Senate. I appreciate the opportunity, and all of our witnesses.

The Olympic Games have great potential, as they embody the greatness of the human spirit, to give us an opportunity to look, as they should, at what it means to be part of the human community. The issue of human rights obviously needs to be at the center of that.

This commission and this body—and I would say the American people—take very seriously that responsibility to look at it as a world citizen and understanding what is there. I have had the opportunity to live and work amongst my Chinese friends, and having been in China during Tiananmen Square and after, understanding that that spirit is there amongst the Chinese people, too.

There is a sense of responsibility for us to probe deeply as a people, looking at the Games and letting those Olympic Games be a mirror to us also. The Universal Declaration of Human Rights that this nation was party to in 1947, there are some core beliefs there that I think, by asking these questions about the Olympics, by asking these questions how the Chinese Government is fulfilling their responsibility to their people, lets us as a human nation get beyond some of these sticking points and get to some true solutions.

So I thank the Chairman for the opportunity to be here, and thank the witnesses.

Chairman LEVIN. Thank you.

Mr. Royce?

STATEMENT OF HON. EDWARD R. ROYCE, A U.S. REPRESENTATIVE FROM CALIFORNIA, MEMBER, CONGRESSIONAL-EXECUTIVE COMMISSION ON CHINA

Representative ROYCE. Thank you, Mr. Chairman. I appreciate the opportunity to serve on this commission. I think the Olympic Games have put a light on China. It is soon going to be a spotlight. I think many of us have come to view China's hosting of these Games as some pretty key leverage in pushing for greater press freedom, transparency, and human rights. I think we have to be realistic. I think Secretary Rice put it well the other day. "Let us not get carried away,"she said, "with what listening to Dvorjak is going to do in North Korea."

I think the same could be said of the Olympics in Beijing. The Games are going to come and go, and they are going to go pretty quickly. It is the long-term impact that we are interested in.

I want to give one example, Mr. Chairman. It was announced today that, sensitive of its image leading up to the Games, China will resume its human rights dialogue with the United States, and that is very positive. Yet, we have heard that commitment before. We need to make sure that this isn't an empty promise that disappears after those closing ceremonies.

I would also like just to point out that this commission has been working on an issue which I hope we continue to work on. This is an issue that humanitarians here have brought to us, working on behalf of North Korean refugees inside China. There are a number of North Korean refugees in China under UNHCR protection, yet China has refused to issue them an exit visa unless the UNHCR agrees not to process any more asylum seekers until after the Beijing Olympics are over.

Now, I understand that China's policy is now undermining the UNHCR's ability to bring additional refugees into protection. Mr. Chairman, this is unacceptable. These refugees could be quickly resettled in third countries. China knows this, we know it. I hope that this is an issue that the Commission can further explore, and I thank you again, Mr. Chairman, Co-Chairman, for your good work here on the Commission.

Chairman LEVIN. Mr. Honda?

Representative HONDA. Thank you, Mr. Chairman, for allowing us to speak. I will yield my time to you and to our witnesses so we can get on with the program.

Chairman LEVIN. Mr. Manzullo?

Representative MANZULLO. I have no statement. I ask that my written statement be entered into the record.

Chairman LEVIN. All right.

We are going to begin. The bell has rung. But Mr. Dorgan will carry on.

I think what I will do, is introduce the five of you, and again, thank you. The focus of this hearing is on human rights and the rule of law in China. That is the basic purview of this commission. That has really determined the kind of testimony that we want today.

We will first hear from Mr. Martella, who is the General Counsel for the Environmental Protection Agency. Each of you has a long list of accomplishments, but I will just give the titles, if I might.

Sharon K. Hom is the Executive Director of Human Rights in China, and a Professor of Law Emerita at the City University of New York School of Law. I stumbled over emerita; you are much too young. I do not quite understand that.

Bob Dietz. Mr. Dietz is Asia Program Coordinator for the Committee to Protect Journalists [CPJ]. Sophie Richardson is the Asia Advocacy Director of Human Rights Watch. Robin Munro is the Research Director for the China Labour Bulletin.

So, Mr. Co-Chair, take over. We will stay for a few minutes. Is there just one vote? Does anybody know? I hope so.

[The prepared statement of Representative Manzullo appears in the appendix.]

Co-Chairman DORGAN [presiding]. Mr. Martella, thank you very much. Why don't you proceed? Your formal statements will be part of the record. We will ask each of you to summarize your statement now for us.

STATEMENT OF ROGER R. MARTELLA, JR., GENERAL COUNSEL, ENVIRONMENTAL PROTECTION AGENCY, WASHINGTON, DC

Mr. MARTELLA. Chairman Levin, Co-Chairman Dorgan, members of the Commission, thank you for providing me with the opportunity and the honor to appear before you today.

The subject of today's hearing raises issues of critical importance not just to China, but to the world. Beyond the sporting events and pageantry, the Beijing Olympics, more importantly, may offer spectators the broadest window yet into a much more needed feat of strength: has the planet's fastest-growing economy developed the fundamental legal pillars worthy of the world's greatest stage?

After the torch is extinguished in August, international opinion likely will remember less the medals Chinese athletes take home, but more of the nation's achievements—or the lack thereof—on the fundamental issues of human rights, the rule of law, and environmental protection.

I am here today to address China's efforts to provide one of the most vital pillars of human life: a safe, healthy, and clean environment. Environmental leaders and scholars have often framed environmental protection as critical to human rights.

In September 2007, I instituted the EPA China Environmental Law Initiative. The initiative is premised on the experience in the United States that a strong environmental law framework is a critical prerequisite to a strong environment. At the center of our initiative is the only Web site we are aware of dedicated to Chinese environmental laws.

In China, according to the World Bank, between 1981 and 2001 the proportion of those living in poverty fell from 53 percent to 8 percent. While this indisputably is a laudable accomplishment, what is less clear in 2008 is the percentage of those not living in economic poverty, but environmental poverty. To give just one insight regarding air issues alone, particulate levels in Beijing are as much as six times that of New York City.

Reportedly, more than 300,000 people per year die prematurely from air pollution in China. With this backdrop, China is planning to build over 500 coal-fired power plants before 2020. Just today on the Associated Press there was an article: "Pollution Turns China River Red and Foamy, Two Hundred Thousand Lose Water."

In the face of these issues it is important to make one point clear. From my firsthand observations, what China does will make a better environment. Several factors motivate that goal, including the Olympics. As Senator Dorgan recognized a few minutes ago, with the international media presence and all eyes on Beijing this August, China knows the world is watching not just its athletes, but its gray skies as well, and needs to promote a positive image of the environment.

From the beginning, the 2008 Beijing Olympic Games Organizing Committee (BOCOG) has promoted the event as the "Green Olympics." A report from the United Nations last year credited Beijing with significant strides in an investment of $12 billion to improve the environment in advance of the Olympics. At the same time, it recognized significant concerns remaining with air pollution, particularly due to the introduction of 1,000 new car registrations every day in Beijing.

In its own way, the 2008 Beijing Olympics demonstrates both everything China is doing well to provide a healthier environment for its residents and the significant challenges that lie ahead.

First, the Olympics demonstrate China's world-class sophistication and ability to understand, communicate, and address environmental issues and challenges. In other words, the Olympics demonstrate clearly that China possesses the scientific, technical, and financial resources needed to promote a better environment.

Second, the 2008 Olympics demonstrate the government's flexibility, prioritizing environmental concerns and targeting solutions toward those concerns. However, questions that must be considered after August include the extent to which, by focusing on an Olympic priority, China merely transported environmental concerns from one area to another, the extent to which this Olympic priority was at the expense of other existing environmental concerns, and to the extent to which the lessons learned in Beijing will be applied elsewhere in China.

Third, critical to convincing the world of a message is the assurance that the message is authentic, that the public trusts it, and that it is enabled to participate through public participation and a transparent process. In this way China has arguably made less progress. The plethora of numbers, criteria, and accomplishments cited by the government frequently come without the transparency we would expect and which are critical to other environmental law frameworks. This, in turn, can raise doubts about authenticity. While on the other hand there are some positive trends toward public participation in environmental lawmaking, the pace must improve for the public to have meaningful input.

Finally, perhaps the most significant contribution to the Green Olympics will not be any specific measurable environmental benefit, but hopefully an awakening to a new approach toward achieving both economic success and environmental protection long-term, as Commissioner Royce suggested as well, looking for long-term solutions.

Beyond specific solutions for a single event, what is more sorely needed are approaches on a national scale. This will require a system of cooperative federalism that encourages local governments to realize and achieve the goals of a clean nation.

The PRC could overcome its most significant hurdle by holding local governments accountable for environmental protection in addition to pure gross domestic product [GDP]. We may begin to see improvements in these lines in the coming months, but I believe this remains the most significant hurdle to a clean environment today in China.

Clearly, the Olympics have brought environmental improvements to the residents of Beijing. What the 2008 Olympics hopefully will bring to all China is an environmental awakening that it can realize a better environment and economic prosperity as mutually achievable and not exclusive goals.

Thank you, Mr. Chairman and Mr. Co-Chairman.

[The prepared statement of Mr. Martella appears in the appendix.]

Co-Chairman DORGAN. Mr. Martella, thank you very much.

Next, we will hear from Ms. Hom. We will again encourage you to know that your entire statements are part of the record, and we will ask you to summarize.

STATEMENT OF SHARON K. HOM, EXECUTIVE DIRECTOR, HUMAN RIGHTS IN CHINA, PROFESSOR OF LAW EMERITA, CITY UNIVERSITY OF NEW YORK SCHOOL OF LAW, NEW YORK, NY

Ms. HOM. Congressman Levin, Senator Dorgan, and members of the Commission, thank you for this opportunity to engage in both the discussion and question and answer session afterward. It is an honor to testify alongside of the distinguished experts and my human rights colleagues on this panel.

With only about five months left to the opening of the Games, we appreciate the Commission's timely attention to the issue, and the rule of law issues as well. We particularly welcome the Commission's "2007 Annual Report," which not only called for an end to the harassment of activists like Hu Jia and other activities, but also raised the really important issues that we will be continuing to discuss today.

There have already been references to the Beijing-specific Olympic obligations, but I would like to put these obligations and promises, and the issue of whether these Olympic promises will lead to any lasting impact, within a broader framework of China's international obligations, including its international human rights obligations.

Additionally, the Olympic obligations and the international obligations are implemented in relationship to domestic Chinese law, in particular, the provisions of the Chinese Constitution, which does include provisions for protecting freedom of speech, press, assembly, association, privacy, correspondence, and the right to criticize the government. So I think that that is the normative universe for assessing the promises. They do not exist in isolation. They did not exist in isolation prior to, during, or after the Olympics. That is the way we can think about leverage for lasting structural change.

Another key rule of law issue is that many of the substantive and legal reforms that have been referenced, including the Open Government initiatives [OGI], and some others that I believe my colleagues will also be talking about, have mostly been formal, law on the books. The real question is implementation.

There are two implementation challenges. One is the hostility of the Chinese authorities to any international or domestic human rights-related criticism, especially criticism related to the Olympics, because the Chinese authorities have characterized any questioning of government policies in the lead-up to the Games as an attack on China itself. This intolerance of criticism and related nationalism conflates China with the Chinese Government.

A government ready to host a major international event, a mature government that respects the rule of law, needs to demonstrate a much higher tolerance for thoughtful, critical, and difficult individual decisions of the conscience. Instead, for example, the recent response by the Chinese authorities to Steven Spielberg's decision was to dismiss him as "naive and foolish."

Domestically, as has already been referenced, there are cases of individuals who are in detention and in prison for raising Olympics-related criticisms. Many are being charged with incitement to subvert state power, with procedural consequences; criminal procedural protections that had been introduced as part of the criminal procedure reforms back in 1997 are no longer available to those charged with subversion or state secrets crimes, resulting in limited access to your lawyer, family, the evidence, and an open trial.

Underlying these implementation issues is a rhetorical zero tolerance for critical voices, despite guarantees in China's own Constitution.

Going forward, a rule of law must be built on accountability and an effective response to the justice claims of the past. Today, at the request of the Tiananmen Mothers, a group within China composed of the families of the victims of June 4th, Human Rights in China [HRIC] is releasing an open letter from the Tiananmen Mothers calling for justice in the lead-up to the Olympics. These brave individuals have made it quite clear that the authorities must address the past if China is to move forward. I would ask that the full text of the Tiananmen Mothers' open letter be entered into the record.

Co-Chairman DORGAN. Without objection.

[The letter appears in the appendix.]

Ms. HOM. Thank you.

The Tiananmen Mothers' open letter states eloquently, "The disastrous aftermath of that brutal massacre, one of the greatest tragedies of our times, even after 18 years is still unresolved. The wounds deep in the heart of the people are not healed. Because of this, the current political and societal landscape continues to deteriorate into disorder and imbalance. This proves that June 4th, this bloody page in history, has yet to be turned and remains a knot deep inside the people's heart."

The letter calls on the Chinese authorities to meet face-to-face and to dialogue with the Tiananmen Mothers. This is a first-time request. In light of the Chinese authorities' recent openness to dialogue with the United States, we would urge and encourage them to also dialogue with their own people.

The Tiananmen Mothers clearly link the human rights issues with the Olympics, asking, "When the government has repeatedly refused dialogue with the victims' families, how can it face the whole world? Is it really possible that as the host of the 2008 Olympic Games the government can be at ease allowing athletes from all over the world to tread on this blood-stained soil and participate in the Olympics?"

So let me take the remaining minute to wrap up and highlight some of the suggestions and questions and concerns that we have. HRIC is not calling for a boycott, as we believe that the hosting of the Games still presents an opportunity and the responsibility to get some traction on the human rights issues and to advance rule of law.

This is up to each of the different actors within our respective sectors: governments, athletes, sponsors, tourists, business people, corporate leaders, and academic exchange programs. For example, a number of journalism and media programs have initiated exchange programs to send journalism students to the BOCOG to help them draft their English-language media work. I would suggest that some important areas to examine include focusing on the orientation for these students, and what kinds of actual media assistance are being offered. We also urge the U.S. Government to continue to raise individual cases at high-level visits and other fora with the Chinese authorities. This sends very clear messages of support. Secretary Rice's recently reported engagement and raising of the case of Hu Jia and other activists is a good example.

We would also like to enter into the record the list of 12 individual rights defenders that Human Rights in China's Olympics Take Action Campaign has featured. These 12 individuals include Shi Tao, Chen Guangcheng, and Mao Hengfeng for March, who has been in detention as a result of violating the one-child population policy. Collectively, these 12, imprisoned for rights-related work, represent the full range of human rights issues addressed by the Campaign.

Regarding these 12 individuals, at least 5 of them have received decisions from the United Nations Working Group on Arbitrary Detention—an international, independent human rights body—that their detentions are arbitrary and in violation of international human rights law. Therefore, urging their immediate releases could not be rejected as interference in the internal matters of China.

Co-Chairman DORGAN. Ms. Hom, we will include those materials in the record. I want to ask you to summarize your statement so that we can get on with the other witnesses.

[The list appears in the appendix.]

Ms. HOM. Thank you.

With respect to censorship and surveillance, we urge the Commission to monitor two areas of concern presented by the security preparations and technology: first is the appropriate balancing of security concerns and protections for human rights—the Johannesburg Principles set forth relevant and appropriate standards; and the other is the post-Olympic use of the advanced security technology that has already been implemented, because there are post-Olympic use provisions in the host city contracts of other cities.

Finally, we would urge the Commission to publicly express your support for the Tiananmen Mothers and other domestic rights defenders. Despite the dismissals of June 4th as belonging to the past by the International Olympic Committee [IOC] president and others, June 4th does not belong to the past, and a peaceful resolution of it will enable a successful future.

Thank you.

[The prepared statement of Ms. Hom appears in the appendix.]

Co-Chairman DORGAN. Ms. Hom, thank you very much for being here, and thank you for your testimony.

Next, we will hear from Mr. Dietz.

Mr. Dietz, you may proceed.

STATEMENT OF ROBERT DIETZ, ASIA PROGRAM COORDINATOR, COMMITTEE TO PROTECT JOURNALISTS, NEW YORK, NY

Mr. DIETZ. Thank you very much for this opportunity. Let me cut right to the chase. China is the world's largest jailer of journalists, and it has held that record since 1999. Currently, CPJ counts 25 journalists behind bars. It is interesting to note that that number is down from 29 of last year and 31 of the year before.

Those raw numbers might make you think that there is a downward trend going on, but in fact what we see is that in China, with the state having advanced its censorship capacity to such a level, that very few journalists, frankly, are willing to take a risk. They are operating in a very commercialized and competitive atmosphere, though, and they continue to push the limits of news coverage.

Let me address our greatest fear in terms of journalism and journalists going into the Olympic Games. It is not the 25,000 to 35,000 foreign journalists who will go to China. Our greatest fear is the Chinese journalists who will find themselves in a heady, new, freer atmosphere, at least in terms of ability for foreign journalists to operate, and that those local journalists might suffer consequences once the spotlight of the Games moves on.

Specifically, we are calling on the foreign media companies which are going to China and will be hiring hundreds, and most likely several thousands, of young people to assist them as production assistants, runners, gofers, drivers, translators, people who can arrange meetings.

We want international media to be aware that the rules under which they are allowed to operate at this point in China, which have been liberalized, do not apply to the Chinese journalists. And that especially when you are dealing with younger people who will be working for these foreign media companies, we want to impress upon them that they must take into concern the fact that even though these young people will be eager to follow orders to try and prove themselves to their new employers, they are doing that at some degree of risk. The one thing we are trying to impress on all of our colleagues in the media is, frankly, to be very aware of that.

Ms. Hom ran down the way that the Chinese use state subversion laws to jail people. That is also the case with journalists, too. More than one-half of the journalists in jail are behind bars because of similar charges. The charge varies at times, but basically "state security" is the catch-all phrase that lets the judge throw the book at a journalist.

It is also interesting to note that more than half of the journalists in jail are imprisoned because of Internet-related activities. When we look at the Internet in China, we see a very dynamic situation. There is still a battle being fought between the government and people who would seek to make use of the Internet and its free speech capabilities as is done in much of the West.

The jury is out on who will win that technological battle. I think what we see on the Internet now is a drive from underneath, people using the Internet in rural villages in protests and factory strikes, places where the local government has come down and tried to suppress dissent. It is on the Internet that we see the source material from the grassroots that tends to rise up, and at times gets covered in mainstream Chinese media.

We have three journalists who are due to be released sometime before the Games start in August. It would be a significant gesture on their part to release them immediately. We really think that at this point China has to begin to move ahead on these sorts of issues.

We are pleased to see that all of a sudden a door, an apparent window of opportunity, is opening in which our government will engage with them on pressing these issues. In my longer testimony I have supplied the names of the three journalists who are due out. Frankly, we think it should be more than just the three. All 25 should be released. But we are ready to take this just one step at a time.

It is also interesting to note that China is in a race with Cuba to be the world's largest jailer of journalists. It would be great if China were to lose that race to the bottom, to lose that perverse contest.

I will end my remarks fairly quickly. All the people that you see at this table know each other. We work together. We have had this challenge on our plate for a couple of years now. We saw the period as a window of opportunity. We jumped on it. Last year we prepared this report, "Falling Short," and we are revising it for release again this year, detailing how China controls journalists.

So, to the extent that we have seen any change, we would like to think that we have had a role in that and their activities. But, frankly, there has not been that much. The situation for media in

China is nowhere near what was promised by either the IOC or the Chinese Government back in 2001 when they assured everyone that this would be a much better situation. It is just not.

I think we all agree that we have to call on you, the members of this commission, and the members of our governments to begin to bring this pressure, as well as us. We have done what we can. We are going to continue to do this. But at some point the onus falls on you as well.

In doing that advocacy, we hope that in addition to pressuring China specifically on these media issues, that you take on the International Olympics Committee, who entered into an agreement in 2001 with the Chinese Government, reassured everyone over very loud complaints, a very loud expression of concern, about what would happen. They said, don't worry, this is a done deal and it is going to work. Well, it is nowhere near working and it certainly seems like it is not going to change in any significant or acceptable way by the August Games.

You have my testimony. I think I have hit the high spots, and I am ready to allow others to speak and use up any time that is left over.

[The prepared statement of Mr. Dietz appears in the appendix.]

Co-Chairman DORGAN. Mr. Dietz, thank you——

Congressman Levin has rejoined us. Perhaps——

Chairman LEVIN. No, keep going.

Co-Chairman DORGAN. We will continue with Ms. Richardson.

Chairman LEVIN. And we have, fortunately, a Motion to Recommit. Hopefully, they will take the full 10 minutes, and then we will have 15 minutes to vote. So if each of you could, take five minutes if possible and then let us do some questioning. Okay. Thank you.

STATEMENT OF SOPHIE RICHARDSON, ASIA ADVOCACY DIRECTOR, HUMAN RIGHTS WATCH, WASHINGTON, DC

Ms. RICHARDSON. Thank you. I will be brief.

Chairman Levin, Co-Chairman Dorgan, thank you very much for inviting Human Rights Watch to join you today. This is a timely hearing and it is always a privilege to participate with such other distinguished panelists.

There are three key questions before us today. The first, is whether the human rights situation in advance of the 2008 Beijing Games is improving as the Chinese Government has repeatedly insisted it would. We regretfully submit that it is not.

Over the past year we have continued to document not only chronic human rights abuses such as the restrictions on speech, assembly, and participation, but also abuses that are taking place specifically because of the Games. Those issues are discussed at length in our written testimony.

The second question is whether this negative impact will be a lasting one. Human Rights Watch believes that these abuses constitute a failure of the Chinese Government to fulfill its own voluntary promises to improve rights in order to win the bid to host the Olympics, and that unless significant pressure is brought to bear, we fear the negative impact will not only be very difficult to reverse, but it will also mean that in effect the international community will have tacitly endorsed the repression necessary to engineer this particular vision of a modern cosmopolitan China that the Chinese Government so badly wants to portray.

The third question, therefore, is what we can do to alter the current situation to ensure a better outcome. Senator Dorgan, in your opening remarks you suggested your hope that what got discussed today in the messages of this hearing would be heard by the Chinese Government. We think it is equally important to explain to the Chinese people what exactly the U.S. Government is going to do to help defend their human rights.

The Administration and the State Department assure us that they are constantly raising these human rights concerns, and while we applaud those efforts—we really do—we question the efficacy of quiet diplomacy and the absence of more public measures. After all, the decreasing volume of U.S. criticism of China's rights record over the past decade is in part to blame for the current situation.

We are encouraged by Secretary Rice's public discussions in Beijing about specific rights concerns and we strongly urge similar efforts over the coming months. The Chinese Government desperately wants a positive international assessment of its country during this time of unprecedented scrutiny and we believe that, if pressed, it will make progress in order to get such positive reviews, particularly from the United States.

To that end, we respectfully urge a number of steps, including that all Members of Congress and senior Administration officials who visit China in the coming months speak publicly about human rights abuses, and when security for all involved can be assured, that you visit those under house or actual arrest for challenging the Chinese Government.

Second, we urge that the members of this commission request public assurances, particularly from U.S.-based Olympic sponsors, that their business practices in China do not contribute to rights abuses.

Third, that the Administration be asked to articulate how it will respond to rights abuses in the coming months, particularly how it is prepared to assist American journalists who themselves are harassed, detained, or abused while trying to take advantage of the new freedoms that Bob spoke about a moment ago.

Fourth, we ask that the Administration describe what specific rights-promoting activities the President will engage in while he is in Beijing this summer to demonstrate that his rhetorical commitments will in fact be made real. These could include making himself available for online discussions to underscore the importance of Internet freedom, attending the trials of dissidents who have been charged with inciting state subversion, visiting unregistered churches to emphasize the right to practice religion freely, or speaking publicly about the constraints under which Chinese journalists continue to be forced to operate.

Fifth, we urge that if the United States agrees to China's proposal to resume the bilateral human rights dialogues, which at the moment certainly appear like a fairly cynical gesture from Beijing given the timing of this offer, that the United States insist on including the kinds of timelines and benchmarks that were absent from past dialogues and that would have made them much more meaningful exercises.

Finally, we urge that if the current crackdown shows no sign of abating in the current months that you ask the Administration to publicly reconsider whether it is appropriate for the President and other senior members of the Administration to attend the opening or closing ceremonies of the Games. If steps like these are not taken and taken soon, the U.S. Government does run the risk of giving imprimatur of approval to the Chinese Government's rights record.

Thank you very much for the opportunity to participate. I will yield my time to Robin.

[The prepared statement of Ms. Richardson appears in the appendix.]

Co-Chairman DORGAN. Dr. Munro, you may proceed. Thank you very much.

STATEMENT OF ROBIN MUNRO, RESEARCH DIRECTOR, CHINA LABOUR BULLETIN, HONG KONG, CHINA

Mr. MUNRO. Thank you, Mr. Chairman. It is a pleasure to be invited to testify at this important hearing today.

The focus of my comments will be on China's current labor rights situation in general, and I would like to broaden this theme somewhat to address the wider range of human rights and labor rights problems faced by ordinary, non-elite members of society, or what we at China Labour Bulletin in Hong Kong sometimes call human rights for the millions. These are the issues, the rights-related, deeper social issues which will be with us during and long after the Olympics.

But, first, on the Olympics, on the question of whether the upcoming Olympics will or may bring lasting benefits to Chinese citizens and have a positive impact on human rights, I think only one conclusion is possible. We have heard the evidence from my colleagues in the human rights community here today and I will not repeat that.

Basically, the official record to date, I think, makes a mockery of Beijing's pledges to the IOC and to the world, that holding the Games would advance the human rights cause in China. I have been following human rights in China for many years, and even I was surprised at the flagrant and unrestrained way in which the authorities have dealt with dissent or potential dissent in the run-up to the Games. I think anything that moves on the human rights front is going to be taken down.

Clearly, Beijing 2008 is not going to be anything like Seoul 1988. I think it is possible that Beijing may produce a human rights trump card or pull a rabbit out of the hat on the eve of the Olympics, for example, by announcing ratification of the International Covenant on Civil and Political Rights [ICCPR], although that is a long shot, or by more probably releasing one or more high-profile political prisoners.

We have just seen today the announcement that the U.S.-China human rights dialogue will resume. I think, as much as I wish the renewed dialogue well, I think it is a ploy by Beijing. Things like this are used as a smokescreen to deflect international attention away from the continuing Games-related crackdown on civil liberties. Given the severity of that current clamp-down, all these gestures I have mentioned, I think, would be left as hollow and meaningless.

The real danger, though, I think, is that the tight social and political controls set in place for the upcoming Olympics will, once the Games are over, simply become the new normal in China's internal security regime. If that happens, the Games will actually have set the clock back on human rights and civil liberties there.

The government tries nowadays to project two images to the world. One is of the harmonious society, and the other, through the Olympics, is "One World, One Dream." The reality, though, is that China today is very far from being harmonious and it embodies two very different worlds and dreams. On the one hand, there are the dreams and the world of the rising new elite, who enjoy unfettered access to all the best things in life. On the other, you have those of the ordinary people, hundreds of millions of citizens who have no meaningful vote and whose main dream is somehow to make ends meet for the family until the next payday. In the government's view, though, if the desired social harmony cannot be achieved through consensus, then it must be enforced by repression, by silencing popular discontent and demands.

So what, then, are the main long-term social justice, or human rights for the millions, issues I mentioned? Here are a few key examples. First, I think the country's medical care system needs to be completely redesigned to make it more accessible and available to ordinary citizens. For at least the past decade, the cost of medical treatment has been prohibitive for ordinary Chinese citizens, even in the cities. Under the present system, a major illness can bankrupt an entire family within weeks.

Second, the rural education system needs to be completely overhauled and properly funded. School fees are often extremely high, and the result is that poor rural families increasingly cannot afford to keep their children in school for the full nine-year period of compulsory education. So, child labor is on the rise in many parts of the country today. I think, after more than a decade of 10-percent-plus annual GDP growth, the government's failure to make a priority of providing decent medical care and rural education for its citizens is deplorable.

Third, the entrenched problem of official corruption which is now endemic at every level of the administration. Corruption by local officials is at the root of almost every major social injustice and protest issue in the country today and is deeply resented by the great majority of ordinary citizens.

Fourth, the basic livelihood of hundreds of millions of urban and rural workers and their families needs to be guaranteed and protected in terms of access to proper employment, enforcement of legal minimum pay and maximum working hours, and provision of safe working conditions. The appalling situation in China's coal mines, where several thousand miners die needlessly each year as a result of mine bosses' disregard for workplace safety, is only the most dramatic example. The construction industry is another.

The only effective remedy for these workplace problems is for workers to be allowed to form effective self-protection organizations. Trade unions would be the most obvious form, but while legal prohibitions on such groups persist, workers should at least be allowed to form front-line work safety committees and to engage in real collective bargaining with their employers aimed at negotiating minimally acceptable terms and conditions of employment.

All these are the real factors promoting social and political instability in China today, not, as the Chinese Government claims, the dissidents, the civil rights lawyers, and the massively over-exploited migrant workers who are increasingly getting up and protesting.

I think the international community has less and less real influence nowadays over Beijing, on how it treats its citizens, because of China's economic rise and so forth. But does this mean that future prospects for human rights and great social justice in China are bleak? Perhaps surprisingly, I would argue not. The other side of the story is that we are finally seeing, after several decades of economic reform, the emergence of new domestic social forces in China that may well have the will and potential to transform the country's governance from the inside and from the bottom up.

I am thinking of two things, mainly. One, there is now a recognizable worker's rights movement of considerable size taking shape in China, something scarcely conceivable just a decade ago. Tens of thousands of mass labor protests and other acts of worker unrest are taking place across the country each year, despite the strict legal prohibition on trade unions.

These protests are spontaneous. They are not coordinated or interconnected, but they are having a real and tangible effect in promoting greater respect by employers for the country's own labor laws. China's workers, especially the 150 million or so migrant workers, are now clearly on the move. They are no longer playing the role of passive victim to China's economic success story. Instead, they are standing up for themselves and their rights.

And the one-party state, which typically preys on the weak and isolated—the dissidents, the civil rights lawyers, the Falun Gong and others—but fears the strong and numerous, is in turn showing the workers increasing attention and respect as a social force. It is no coincidence that the start of 2008 saw the introduction of three new labor laws in China: the labor contract law, the law on employment promotion, and the law on labor dispute mediation and arbitration. All of these new laws have in significant ways raised the bar on employment standards and labor rights.

Chairman LEVIN [presiding]. Mr. Munro, if you could wrap up quickly to give us time before those darned bells ring again.

Mr. MUNRO. I will, thank you.

The second main force is the rise of the "rights defense movement" in China, to my mind the most hopeful and optimistic sign in the country on the human rights front for decades. For reasons of time, I refer the panel to my written testimony for more information on that.

I would like to conclude by giving several suggestions on what the international community can do to best lend its support to the promising new developments taking place at the grassroots level in China. These developments, I should add, are not ones fostered or initiated by the government, this is ordinary Chinese people taking the initiative, creating the social space, and fighting for their rights against local officials.

First, I think Western governments need to continue to press China to ratify core agreements on freedom of speech and association. This is fundamental. If Chinese citizens cannot freely associate to press for peaceful change and reform, the country will become more and more of a political powder keg on the world stage.

Governments should also continue to press Beijing for the release of individual prisoners of conscience. Human rights dialogue or not, this should now, I think, be put back as a major part of government policy by Western nations.

I think Western foundations should greatly increase the kind of support they give to grassroots-based civic action groups of all kinds in China. As I have indicated, these groups are the country's main hope for the future.

Multinationals operating in China have a moral duty to maintain strong codes of conduct and pursue corporate social responsibility, but social justice in the workplace in China cannot be planned and executed from corporate board rooms and Western capitals. China's workers are quite capable of protecting themselves, given the necessary rights and tools, and there is no shortcut for them doing so.

Finally, I think both multinationals and consumers in the West need to recognize that if acceptable labor standards are to come in China, the cost of China's exported goods will have to rise. These goods are too cheap, and under-priced Chinese goods means continued labor rights violations in China.

In conclusion, China's hosting of the Games may be momentous for reasons of national pride, but I would submit it is largely irrelevant to the real social issues facing China and its people today. Unless these issues are addressed by the government, China's Olympic slogan of "One World, One Dream" will end up being viewed by its people as one more cynical diversion from reality, to be added to the scrap heap of similar slogans used by the party over the past 60 years.

Mr. Chairman, I request, following my written statement, that an article drafted by my colleagues at China Labour Bulletin be included in the hearing record. This is an article to be published in the upcoming book, "China's Great Leap," and it addresses the conditions of migrant workers both at Olympic construction sites and across the country.

Thank you for your time and attention.

Chairman LEVIN. Thank you. Without objection.

[The article appears in the appendix.]

[The prepared statement of Dr. Munro appears in the appendix.]

Chairman LEVIN. We have a vote, but I'm going to ask a question, if you would start discussing it. I don't know that there's any controversy left about the need to engage China. The issue of China's ascendancy to the WTO was very controversial, but with its growth, with its importance, I do not think any longer there is much debate that they are an important part of the international spectrum. This commission was set up as part of that debate to look at human rights issues, including worker rights issues and the rule of law.

Let me just ask you this. I know there are various views as to how our government and our private and public groups should approach these issues of relationship with China, especially human rights, worker rights issues, and rule of law.

I quote one person who was in a previous administration: "It's a striking example," talking about the pressure to raise these issues, "of how single-issue groups of all kinds are trying to use the Olympics to hammer China." Then he goes on to say, "Linking Darfur, for example, to the Olympic Games will not help to resolve this issue. The Chinese tend to respond badly to public pressure."

React to that, what you believe is the appropriate approach—you've commented on it in part. These are key issues, human rights issues, worker rights issues, rule of law. How do we approach these issues, both governmentally and non-governmentally in this country?

Each of you, if you would take a crack at that, I'd give each of you time to discuss it. You've touched on it, but this is one of the nubs. We are holding this hearing on the assumption that it is wise for this to be out in the open, right? That it is wise for Congress to be engaged, it is right for the Administration, which is part of this commission, to be engaged, and you are here, Mr. Martella, as part of it. So just comment on that: what should we do in these next months. You want to go down the line?

Ms. HOM. Thank you. I think it is a difficult question. We hear that a lot from different sectors, the media, the corporate sector, the IOC, and most recently from the foreign media representative for BOCOG, who had the misfortune, or fortune, to be on the same panel with me on a recent NPR program. He essentially denied that there are human rights problems in China and claimed the list of human rights issues I outlined—media control and censorship, attacks on defenders, etc.—was "hogwash." What is appropriate to expect? I think what we would begin with, what is appropriate, totally appropriate is to expect of the Chinese authorities what they themselves have promised, what they promised the international community, what they have promised to their own people, and what China has promised to its Olympic Movement partners, its government partners, et cetera.

Second, it is important that there be respect for diverse approaches, which is not in the Chinese official universe.

Finally, on engagement, apropos of the resumption of dialogue—and I want to align myself with many of the comments that have already been made on the panel—any dialogue that is resumed between the United States and China needs to really be much more transparent to the public.

Perhaps two lessons from the EU-China dialogue might be kept in mind. While the EU-China human rights dialogue does have publicly announced benchmarks, the benchmarks have produced limited results: benchmarks are only as good as the level of transparency, and availability of accurate, reliable, and comprehensive information, and that is a major problem, as we know in China, primarily because of the state secrets framework.

Second, the EU-China human rights dialogue is perhaps one of the most advanced and developed ones, along with the Norwegian dialogue, in terms of including different actors, including civil society actors and NGOs. Yet, China has been extremely active in its strategy to throw around its weight and control, to shape the dialogue, and to exclude the very civil society voices that the EU Government is trying to include. Most recently, China's efforts to exclude China Labour Bulletin and Human Rights in China from the Human Rights dialogue seminar in Berlin, and then walking out, is instructive.

Chairman LEVIN. All right. Good.

Mr. Dietz, if you would, all of you, briefly comment. Then after, Mr. Smith and I have to leave and Mr. Dorgan is going to wrap things up.

Mr. DIETZ. I will give you the advice of my high school defensive football coach who said, "Hit 'em high, hit 'em low." CPJ engages many countries, not just China, on these sorts of issues. At times we pull back for fear of jeopardizing someone's safety, other times we are very vocal, other times we play a balance.

I was in Hong Kong at the beginning of last month, sitting around the Foreign Correspondence Club with a bunch of journalists from the Hong Kong Journalists Association, and I said there are times when I'm not sure that I am doing anything of value and that I am just making things worse for people in jail. Their response was, if CPJ does not speak out, then who will?

There was a journalist released just at the beginning of February, Ching Chong, a Singapore Straits Times reporter who had been held in jail for five years on state subversion charges, state security violations. His wife had been very active over the years, sometimes calling out, sometimes asking us to make statements, other times withdrawing. When we were having our annual press conference in Hong Kong in February, this year she said, "Bob, not this year. We're getting a message that Ching might get out." Sure enough, the day after that he was released and he is now free to walk around in Hong Kong on parole.

I think, in dealing with China, that sensible engagement around these issues is important. And specifically, given the opportunity that we got with the IOC agreement with China about media freedom issues, this is the time to push to fix these things. It was a pledge that was made to the international community, to all of us. I think we have an opportunity to demand that these things be fixed—and we have a right to demand it of China and the IOC.

Chairman LEVIN. You emphasized, as Sharon Hom did, the commitments that were made in fulfillment. Mr. Martella, I don't know if you, before Mr. Smith and I have to leave and Mr. Dorgan takes over to finish, whether you feel comfortable saying something. If so, please do.

Mr. MARTELLA. Well, thank you, Mr. Chairman. I actually think you raise a very important question that I get in a different format, which is why, from an environmental perspective, should EPA or my office care about these issues. I commend the Commission for recognizing the important relationship between environmental issues and human rights issues.

Briefly, I give three reasons. One is a purely altruistic reason, which is, we've learned our lessons here in creating a strong environment in the United States, and we should share that with developing countries and help them do the same. The less altruistic reason is that what happens in China affects us here. Thirty percent of the particulate matter in the West is created in China, 25 percent of the world's mercury emissions come from China.

They are the largest polluter in the Pacific Ocean. They are close, if not beyond us, as a greenhouse gas emitter for climate change, and they have a tremendous thirst for energy, as well as, we are concerned about imports, including lead in toys from China, so we should be concerned about gauging what is happening there as it affects us.

Then the third reason pertains to multinationals, both organizations and companies that are operating there as a matter of doing business in the global world. January 31, 2008, China issued a press release that they are bringing 130 multinationals to the book, and these are their words, "for breaking environmental protection laws," but the press release is very vague and ambiguous.

So I do think it is important from an environmental perspective, as you say, that we gauge what is happening there, both because we want to help advance the environment there, which probably should be a primary concern, but also because it does affect both people and organizations here in the United States.

Chairman LEVIN. We have, Mr. Smith and I, just five minutes. After I leave, if you would also put this in the context of the Beijing Games. I think it is important for us to ask ourselves, in terms of our efforts, whether it is appropriate—which I think it is—to use this opportunity to ask China—to insist—that they fulfill their commitments. I will tell them to hold open the vote.

Representative SMITH of New Jersey. Thank you very much, Mr. Chairman. I would like to ask a couple of questions, very briefly, through you, Mr. Chairman. I thank you for yielding.

A couple of points; this commission was formed to be kind of a carbon copy of the Helsinki Commission. I chaired that commission for 12 years, and have been on it for 26 of my 28 years as a Member of Congress. It works because of the engagement. When the Eastern Bloc and the Soviet Union were absolutely intransigent, we were able to get concessions, political prisoners out because we had some economic leverage. We had a lot of things going for us.

Unfortunately, a lot of the economic leverage has been forfeited with the permanent normal trade relations [PNTR], in my opinion, and we have little more than moral suasion left in our quiver. They do not get held to account by the United Nations. I remember after Wei Jingsheng got out of prison, I was in China during his release when the Beijing Government was vying for the 2000 Olympics. I met with him for three hours before he got rearrested and then was brutally beaten, as we all know. When he was let out, his first stop was my committee room. I chaired the Human Rights Committee.

He reiterated what he told me in that dinner conversation. He said, this is counter-intuitive, but when you make nice and when you, America and Europe, clank the champagne glasses, they beat us more. But when you're tough and consistent, they get the message that you mean business and they beat us less. That's when prisoners may find release.

Your thoughts on that would be appreciated. Like the Chairman, I am going to have to go for a vote, or the second one, because I'll miss this one. But the idea of soft diplomacy, it needs to be very consistent and strong and equally applied over and over and over again—but I'm more for just total transparency.

I remember when Frank Wolf and I met with Li Peng. We gave him a list of prisoners. He wouldn't even touch it. But he was so incensed by it that he brought it up the next day. Then we heard that some of the people got more lenient treatment. Now, we cannot for sure prove it, but we have to be bolder, but diplomatic. I think, unfortunately, we have squandered a lot of that.

Second, on the labor issue, a year ago Ben Cardin and I went on record on an AFL–CIO complaint that was extremely well written about labor issues. Dr. Munro, you might want to answer this. The USTR would not even take it up. I mean, 10 to 15 cents per hour, 126,000 people killed; that is what they report that could have been prevented if they had OSHA-type protections. All the litany of problems, just on the labor rights issue. They wouldn't even take it up. I hope it is not a lost opportunity. Unfair labor is against our law. I hope that maybe this commission could pressure the USTR to take that up anew. Maybe your comments on that would be helpful.

The venues for the Olympics; have any of them been made with gulag labor? I was just in Kinshasa in DR Congo for a week. I went to a place where there is a huge Chinese effort of building and I was told—and we have not verified it yet—but the suspicion is that some of those who were working at that venue, at that building, are gulag labor. Harry Wu has testified many times about how forced labor is endemic. But are any of the Olympic venues made by gulag labor? If not gulag labor, were those who worked on the stadiums and the track and field aspects of it paid? What was the situation there? I think it is a very valid question.

Ms. Hom, you might want to touch on the issue, if you could, briefly, of the missing girls in China. I said it at the opening. Very often, the human rights community has been mum on the fact that the family has been violated with impunity. Women have been raped by the state. Forced abortion is rape. It is horrible. It is used with particular impunity against the Uighurs, against the Tibetans, and against girls.

The Chinese Government loves to say they have this policy or that policy. Since 1998 or 1999, they've been saying we signed the International Covenant for Civil and Political Rights, usually when one of their heads of state are heading to our shores, so that it allays concerns, just like the resumption of the human rights dialogue. So perhaps, Ms. Hom, you could speak to the issue of this terrible crime of missing girls.

One demographer in China has said, by the year 2020, 40 million men will not be able to find a wife because, since 1979, systematically girls have been targeted for extinction. It is genocide, gendercide, and it is only going to get worse. It will exacerbate human trafficking because it will become a magnet, the dearth of women, the disproportion will lead to horrible consequences. So, if you could touch on that.

Finally, some of you might want to speak to the issue of global online freedom. I know, Sophie Richardson, your organization has strongly endorsed it.

Co-Chairman DORGAN [presiding]. I am going to ask now, since you have got about eight questions on the table here that we have the witnesses respond in writing to some of them.

Representative SMITH of New Jersey. That would be good.

Co-Chairman DORGAN. I have limited time as well. I have to go back to the Senate in a few moments.

But why don't we have Ms. Hom respond to the question that you just asked about the women.

Ms. HOM. Very quickly, and we can submit some additional information. I had mentioned that HRIC's Take Action Campaign for the Olympics features an individual every month. The woman we are featuring in March is Mao Hengfeng, who has been tortured, detained, beat up, and subjected to all kinds of abuse. She is currently serving a two-and-a-half-year prison sentence for breaking a lamp. She is one example of a particularly draconian and coercive implementation of the one-child population policy.

On the Campaign Web site, *www.ir2008.org,* in addition to finding out more about her case, there are also issue backgrounders, both from the perspective of women's health and women's rights, and the issue of petitioners, because Mao Hengfeng is an example of the thousands of petitioners who exercise their right to petition and then face detention and abuse. Finally, one of the main reasons, in addition to the economic reasons, that this policy continues is the devaluation of female life. The value of female life is not as "a future wife"—that has to change.

Representative SMITH of New Jersey. Right. Excellent.

Co-Chairman DORGAN. Mr. Smith, you have a long history of passionate care and concern about these issues and I hate to cut you short.

Representative SMITH of New Jersey. I understand.

Co-Chairman DORGAN. I'd like to ask just two questions.

Representative SMITH of New Jersey. If you could provide that for the record, the other individuals.

Co-Chairman DORGAN. Yes. Let us ask if you would submit for the record——

Representative SMITH of New Jersey. As to the venue, if you could find that out.

[The responses to Representative Smith's questions appear in the appendix.]

Co-Chairman DORGAN. I think you have asked a lot of very important questions and I think we will want responses on the record.

Ms. Hom, do you believe that what you have said here today would make you eligible for a criminal charge, and perhaps jailing, in the country of China were you a resident of China living in China at the time of making these statements?

Ms. HOM. Actually, I have made many of these statements publicly, and I got an interesting hate e-mail on Monday from someone who purports to be Chinese.

Co-Chairman DORGAN. But I'm saying, if you lived in Beijing.

Dr. Munro, would you be jailed in China if you were a Chinese citizen living in Beijing, speaking of the issues you have addressed today?

Mr. MUNRO. Well, my subject today was more labor rights, which is somewhat less controversial. But in general, the things I've said on human rights in China over the years, I have no doubt, yes, my feet wouldn't touch the floor. I'd be straight off to prison.

Co-Chairman DORGAN. Mr. Martella, my understanding is that the steel production in China generates about three times the amount of carbon per ton of production as steel production in the United States. I believe that's the case. I understand that the Chinese have decided to move one of the mammoth steelworks away from Beijing to an island 140 miles or so away from Beijing. Is that correct?

Mr. MARTELLA. That's correct, Senator. Yes.

Co-Chairman DORGAN. So that's the way they deal with air pollution?

Mr. MARTELLA. Well, you raise a very important point. China's greenhouse gas intensity, this is how much greenhouse gases you emit as you produce, say, $1 of GDP, is the highest in the world, even higher than the developing countries as a whole. So they are very energy inefficient and they anticipate that their CO_2 emissions will be going up. They have gone up 80 percent since 1990. They are projected to go up another 65 to 80 percent by 2020.

But you raise a very good point. When I was in Beijing, there were many smokestacks. Virtually all the ones we saw had been shut down. We asked—we would see new industrial facilities built within 10, 15 years ago and we asked, where are the businesses? This is 30 miles outside Beijing. They said they've been relocated. We didn't know where they relocated to, but they've been relocated.

So they have taken incredibly dramatic efforts, including relocating entire industries outside Beijing, to prepare for the Olympics. Having said that, if you were to go there today there is a good chance the air quality would still be quite poor despite those very dramatic efforts to relocate almost entire industries.

Co-Chairman DORGAN. Mr. Martella, I wrote a book a couple of years ago called "Take This Job and Ship It," about shipping jobs overseas. I described in that book the China haze, which is to say that we all live in the same fishbowl, the same environment.

Mr. MARTELLA. Yes.

Co-Chairman DORGAN. What they do in China, we breathe. It is just a matter of fact. I understand, in one of the pieces of testimony I read last evening, they are saying that some athletes preparing for the Olympics are testing their ability to train with face masks, anticipating an air quality problem when they compete. Have you heard of this?

Mr. MARTELLA. That was something we realized earlier this month, that many countries that set up training camps, apparently including the United States, I believe, outside of China so people can fly in at the last minute, they are also testing with dust masks on to give themselves kind of acclimation to what they're anticipating once they get there. My own personal view on this, I am 37 years old. I feel very fortunate having grown up in a country where I have never had ramifications from my environment. The only time that has ever happened was spending a couple days in Beijing. It was the first time in my life where I have actually had physical reactions to the quality of the air.

Co-Chairman DORGAN. From my understanding, this issue of human rights, making progress on human rights, progress on the environment and so on, these are commitments that the Chinese Government itself made, are they not? I mean, is this not the case where, as they ramped up to try to get the International Olympic Committee to select them for the Olympics, they made representations about their commitments with respect to air quality, environment, human rights. Is that right?

Mr. MARTELLA. That is right.

Co-Chairman DORGAN. It is not a case of us saying to the Chinese, look, here's what we expect you to do. It is a case of the Chinese saying, here is what we will do, and now we are saying, when, and why aren't you doing it now? Isn't that right?

Mr. MARTELLA. They held themselves out as the Green Olympics. That's the name they adopted for themselves. To give them credit, they have accomplished a great many things in that time. But at the same time, particularly regarding air quality, they have not achieved the goals. The other questions that remain are, while they may have devoted all these resources toward Beijing and the Olympics, what have they done in other places and what has not been done as a result of prioritizing these resources toward one event?

Co-Chairman DORGAN. Well, all of you, I know, have done a lot of work. Dr. Munro, I am told you are back on an airplane, is it tomorrow, back to Hong Kong? Ms. Richardson, I am very familiar with your organization and the work you do. Mr. Dietz, the journalists are soldiers in search of truth across the world, and many not only risk losing their lives, as some do, but others find themselves in prison for telling the truth and printing the truth.

I really appreciate the work that all of you have done to shed light on these issues before this commission. What we're trying to do is to hold up a mirror and find out what was promised and what has been the result. The fact is, China is going to be a significant part of our future and our lives. The question is, for good or ill? It is a major player on the world stage. We, I think all of us, want the same thing for China and its people. We want greater human rights, we want it through engagement of trade and travel and opportunities such as this one today to move China in a very constructive direction in terms of the way it creates its society, being open and providing opportunities for folks.

I must say, it has been a good many years since I served in the U.S. House and I had forgotten about these bells and how often they vote here. In the U.S. Senate, we do not vote until it gets dark, so you notice I have not been interrupted. But when the sun goes down and it gets dark, we will have Senators show up on the floor demanding votes. That is the way the Senate works.

So my colleagues, I know, feel badly that they had to rush back and forth and back and forth, but you know by the number of people who came at the start of this hearing, we care about this very much. This commission is not just some afterthought, this commission is very important. China is a very important part of the world community. We are very concerned. We have put in the record now I think two lists of Chinese prisoners. We also have a database, I believe, at our Congressional-Executive Commission on China that is the most credible database on those individuals who are held in

Chinese prisons as a result of what we consider to be a violation of human rights.

So we are going to continue this work. We appreciate all of you being willing to take some time from your schedule and to attend this hearing.

This hearing is adjourned.

[Whereupon, at 4:08 p.m. the hearing was adjourned.]

APPENDIX

PREPARED STATEMENTS

_____

PREPARED STATEMENT OF ROGER R. MARTELLA, JR.

FEBRUARY 27, 2008

Chairman Levin, Chairman Dorgan, members of the Commission:

Thank you for providing me the opportunity and the honor to appear before you today.

The subject of today's hearing, "The Impact of the 2008 Olympic Games on Human Rights and Rule of Law in China," raises issues of critical importance not just to China, but to the world. Beyond the sporting events and pageantry, the Beijing Olympics more importantly may offer spectators the broadest window yet into a more needed feat of strength: whether the planet's fastest growing economy has developed the fundamental legal pillars worthy of the world's greatest stage. After the torch is extinguished at the Beijing National Stadium in August, international opinion likely will remember less the medals China's athletes take home than the nation's achievements—or lack thereof—on the fundamental issues of human rights, the rule of law, and environmental protection.

I am here today to address China's efforts to provide one of the most vital pillars of human life—a safe, healthy, and clean environment. Environmental leaders and scholars have often framed environmental protection as critical to human rights. For example, the landmark National Environmental Policy Act provides that Congress recognizes that "each person should enjoy a healthful environment and [that] each person has a responsibility to contribute to the preservation and enhancement of the environment."[1] In 1992 the U.N. Conference on Environment and Development noted that "human beings are entitled to a healthy and productive life in harmony with nature."[2]

With that backdrop, the 2008 Beijing Olympics are providing an extraordinary front row seat to assess China's accomplishments and challenges in providing a safe environment for the world's largest population. Importantly, though, while the Olympics may provide the world with its most vivid snapshots to date of China's environmental efforts preparing for a single event, it likely will be harder to glean China's ability to conquer the challenges facing the nation's environment beyond Beijing in the years and decades to come.

EPA'S CHINA ENVIRONMENTAL LAW INITIATIVE

In September 2007, I instituted the EPA China Environmental Law Initiative after meeting in China with environmental officials, academics, students, nongovernmental organizations, and multinational corporations. The Initiative is premised on the experience in the United States that a strong environmental law framework is the critical prerequisite to a strong environment. In seeking to improve China's environmental laws I identified three reasons why the United States should help China advance its environmental laws, and thus its environment as a whole.

First, the American environmental law framework is the strongest in the world. Implementing the toolbox of environmental protection statutes Congress started passing in the 1970s has resulted in heralded improvements in environmental protection, and safe air, water, and environment for the nation. From an altruistic point of view, we should share this framework and our experience with China to help it develop a thorough framework tailored to its own geographic, economic, and political circumstances.

Second, and perhaps less altruistic, is the reality that what happens in China increasingly affects the environment here in several ways. Air pollution transported from Asia adds to levels of air pollution in the United States—increasing the challenge of air quality and public health protection. Researchers at Harvard University, using models, have estimated that Asia contributes roughly 30 percent of the background sulfate particulate matter in the Western United States.[3] In 2000, China reportedly emitted over 25 percent of the total estimated worldwide human-generated mercury emissions into the atmosphere, contributing to the global pool of atmos-

---

[1] 42 U.S.C. Section 4331(c).

[2] Rio Declaration, Principle 1, June 3–14, 1992.

[3] R. J. Park et al., *Natural and Transboundary Pollution Influences on Sulfate-nitrate-ammonium Aerosols in the United States: implications for policy*, 109 J. OF GEOPHYSICAL RESEARCH (2004).

pheric mercury that circulates around the northern hemisphere and falls out in Asia, North America, and Europe.[4]

Some researchers believe that China already has overtaken the United States as the leading emitter of greenhouse gas emissions while others believe it inevitably will do so in the near term. China's thirst for energy and other resources brings with it environmental consequences across the globe.[5] And less stringent controls over exports such as lead in toys can lead to environmental harms on any continent.

Third, multinational organizations and corporations increasingly are relying on China both as a growing market and a source of products, while NGOs and academics see an increasing need to understand environmental issues in China as well. Ambiguities in the Chinese environmental law framework create unique challenges for those seeking to understand environmental compliance in China. Thus, one goal of the Initiative is to help digest this information in the interest of advancing multinational understanding of the Chinese environmental law framework.

The EPA China Environmental Law Initiative is continuing the dialog between the United States and China, as well as other interested stakeholders, to advance the Chinese environmental law framework. At the center of this initiative is the first website we are aware of dedicated to Chinese environmental law. The website, which can be found at *www.epa.gov/ogc,* is a collaborative effort of institutions in the United States and in China and is available in English and Chinese. In the roughly three months since we started the website, the front page has been viewed over 4000 times.[6] Users have viewed the Chinese translation of the front page over 2700 times.

This April, I will participate with my staff in a second OGC-organized symposium in China, focused on further development and implementation of environmental laws and the need and opportunity for public participation in environmental regulation.

THE STATE OF THE ENVIRONMENT IN CHINA

According to the World Bank, between 1981 and 2001 the proportion of those living in poverty in China fell from 53 percent to 8 percent. While this indisputably is a laudable accomplishment, what is less clear in 2008 is the percentage of those living not in economic poverty, but environmental poverty.

Robert Percival is the director of the acclaimed Environmental Law Program at the University of Maryland Law School, and a collaborative partner in the EPA China Environmental Law Initiative. As he has aptly put it, "the good news is that things have gotten so bad that high officials cannot help but take note."[7] Indeed, the challenge in expressing the state of the environment in China is discerning which of the plethora of bad fact scenarios gives the best understanding of the dire situation.

For example, regarding air issues alone, particulate levels in Beijing are as much as six times that of New York City. Reportedly, more than 300,000 people per year die prematurely from air pollution in China[8] and each year 400,000 new cases of chronic bronchitis are estimated to occur in 11 large Chinese cities.[9] Emissions of sulfur oxides in China are the highest in the world,[10] double the output of the United States in 2006,[11] costing China an estimated 500 billion Yuan (US$60 billion) in damage to buildings, crops, vegetation and human health.[12] Many Chinese

---

[4] David Streets et al. (2004) US Geological Survey China-Mercury Meeting. "Mercury emissions in China: Update."; Elisabeth Pacyna et al., *Global anthropogenic mercury emission inventory for 2000,* 40 ATMOSPHERIC ENVIRONMENT 4048, 4048 (2006).

[5] According to one account, to produce goods worth $10,000, China uses six times the resources used by the United States. See Elizabeth C. Economy, The Great Leap Backward?, FOREIGN AFFAIRS (Sept/Oct 2007).

[6] Each "view" does not necessarily correspond to a separate person: some users undoubtedly viewed the front page more than once.

[7] Robert Percival, *Still Needed: Enforcement, Public Role (Is Chinese Environmental Law up to the Task?),* 22 ENVIRONMENT FORUM 44 (2005).

[8] WORLD HEALTH ORGANIZATION, WORLD HEALTH REPORT 2002 (2002); Clear Water, Blue Skies (World Bank ed., 1997).

[9] ORGANIZATION FOR ECONOMIC CO-OPERATION & DEVELOPMENT, ENVIRONMENTAL PERFORMANCE REVIEWS, CHINA (2007).

[10] Jianguo Liu & Jared Diamond, *China's Environment in a Globalizing World; How China and the rest of the world affect each other,* 435 NATURE 1179 (2005).

[11] SEPA, State of the Environment Report, http://english.sepa.gov.cn/standards—reports/soe/SOE2006/200711/t20071105—112565.htm (China reporting 25,888K metric tons); U.S. EPA, National Emission Inventory, http://www.epa.gov/ttn/chief/trends/trends06/nationaltier1upto2006basedon2002finalv2.1.xls (U.S. reporting 12,490K metric tons).

[12] Li Xinmin, in The China Post (3 August 2006).

citizens breathe air violating Chinese national air quality standards.[13] And, with this backdrop, China is planning to build over 500 coal-fired power plants before 2020.

By way of context and fairness, it should be noted that in the United States there were several decades of rapid economic growth before we as a nation took seriously the challenge of creating an environmental law framework in the face of pressing environmental concerns such as the Cuyahoga River and Love Canal. As described below, China clearly is taking measures to address environmental concerns during its era of rapid economic growth. The question is less the nation's motivation, but rather the sufficiency of its actions.

CHINA'S WILL IS TOWARD A BETTER ENVIRONMENT

At the outset, it is important to make one point clear. From my first hand interactions and observations, China wills a better environment. Several factors are motivating this goal.

First, the 2008 Olympics is putting more than China's athletes on the world stage. With the international media presence and all eyes on the events there, China knows the world is watching not just the athletes, but its gray skies as well. With much of the world a spectator, China wants and needs to use the spotlight to promote a positive image about the nation that makes so many things the world consumes; a positive image that necessarily includes a clean environment.

Second, beyond the Olympics, China is aware that environmental concerns are drawing increasing scrutiny from multinational organizations and corporations. Just as poor labor conditions can lead to bans and boycotts, increasingly there is interest in looking behind products and into factories to ensure items are manufactured in an environmentally sound way. As China grows into an increasing global player in the world economy, it increasingly will be expected to justify a stronger environmental record.

Third, government officials are not shy to express their concern at protests of any sort. Knowing that environmental issues and advocacy are cause for protests and civil unrest, the Chinese government would appear to prefer addressing concerns in the first instance. In 2007, thousands of citizens protested a chemical factory in Xiamen, expressing concerns about leukemia and birth defects. And in June, hundreds of Beijing residents protested the headquarters of the State Environmental Protection Agency itself regarding a waste incinerator. In personal conversations, Chinese officials have been very frank about their motivation to work proactively to address environmental issues to avoid more such unrest in the future.

Fourth, the government officials I have spoken with on this issue expressed concern and motivation for the environmental health of citizens, regardless of other factors. There does seem to be great concern on how to achieve both economic and environmental objectives simultaneously. But I did observe among officials I met a genuine interest in improving the health and well being of residents.

CHINA'S WAY TOWARD A BETTER ENVIRONMENT IS UNCERTAIN

China for many years has taken at least symbolic steps toward adopting the laws that lead to a better environment. For example, since 1992 China has adopted environmental laws addressing air pollution, water pollution, solid waste, and clean energy production. However, many of these critical provisions lack teeth of enforceability. Many of the laws are vague, and more akin to guidance than regulations.[14] Some were largely adopted from other countries without being adapted to China's geographic, economic, and political circumstances.[15] And the role of public participation, which is as essential to environmental laws in the United States as substantive mandates, largely has been overlooked.

In reviewing the nexus between China's environmental law framework and a better environment for China, four themes are apparent which demonstrate both the strengths and weaknesses of the existing Chinese environmental law framework. As discussed below, each of these themes bears relevance to the 2008 Olympics.

First, the Chinese government's understanding and messaging of environmental issues and possible solutions appears to be as sophisticated as any other nation's. When speaking with Chinese officials from the national State Environmental Protection Agency to the local Environmental Protection Bureaus, it is easy to be im-

---

[13] Mun Ho & Chris Nielsen, Cleaning the Air: Health and Economic Damages of Air Pollution in China (MIT Press, 2007) (in 1999, over 200 Chinese cities with air pollution monitors were out of compliance with at least one of the nation's air-quality standards for residential areas).

[14] Alex Wang, *One Billion Enforcers,* 24 ENVIRONMENTAL FORUM (2007).

[15] Country Environmental Analysis for the People's Republic of China, ADB May, 2007.

pressed by the depth of the understanding of environmental concerns, and the ideal solutions needed to address them. So, in short, the messages communicated by the government at all levels on environmental issues are sophisticated and strong.

Second, the government appears to take a pragmatic approach of prioritizing areas of immediate concern and takes steps toward addressing those situations. For example, rather than address air quality generally China might focus on acid rain specifically; rather than address water quality generally China might focus on a specific area of concern such as chemical oxygen demand. Undoubtedly an approach of prioritizing environmental concerns makes common sense. At the same time, though, absent an effective overall framework for addressing broader environmental concerns such as clean air and water generally, a concern lies with whether progress is being made on the plethora of issues not identified as priorities.

Third, one of the significant limitations at this time toward understanding the advancement of environmental protection in China relates to the critical roles that transparency, public participation, and authentication play in environmental law. It is relatively common to hear news in China that some environmental measurement has improved over a period of time. However, observers frequently raise doubts regarding the authenticity of such figures given their inability to "look behind the numbers" at the raw data and challenge the assumptions. This deficiency is compounded by the current presumption of little to no public participation in the lawmaking process, although as described below there is some evidence of progress in this area.

Fourth, and to me the most significant theme inhibiting the implementation of a strong environmental law framework, goes to the lack of a system of cooperative federalism and enforcement in China. In the United States, cooperative federalism is the necessary method by which the network of environmental laws works to ensure a clean environment for all Americans. Our laws work, in general, by delegating primary responsibility to states for implementation and enforcement, but ensuring the Federal Government will enforce a floor of beneficial measures and standards. In China in contrast, the national government has limited mechanisms to ensure its environmental goals at the regional and local level. To the contrary, the national government largely awards local governments and officials based on their increase in GDP, with little or no accountability for environmental protection and harm.[16] To me, the key to creating a strong framework in China is developing a different kind of cooperative federalism there, and thus eliminating this disjointedness between the goals of the national government and the incentives driving the provincial governments. In other words, a key way to implement cooperative federalism in China may be as straightforward as holding government accountable for environmental advancement along with economic growth.

THE 2008 OLYMPICS: A BETTER ENVIRONMENT FOR BEIJING, BUT WHAT ABOUT CHINA?

The Beijing 2008 Olympic Games Organizing Committee promoted the event as the "Green Olympics." Consistent with that commitment, the Organizing Committee has identified scores of efforts to improve the environment in Beijing prior to the Games.[17] These efforts are as basic as improving water quality, upgrading sewer capacity, and promoting tree planting at a Beijing park. Other efforts are radically bold by any standard, including experiments to restrict car traffic by 50 percent on certain days and shuttering and relocating entire industries from greater Beijing, including the transitioning of the mammoth Shougang steel works to an island 139 miles from Beijing.

A report by The United Nations Environment Programme credited Beijing with "significant strides" and an investment of $12 billion to improve the environment in advance of the Olympics.[18] At the same time, it recognized concerns remaining with air quality despite the relocation of industry, particularly due to the introduction of 1,000 new car registrations daily. Indeed, in what may be the most qualitative assessment regarding Beijing's air quality, it was widely reported earlier this month that dozens of countries have set up training camps for the days ahead of the events not in China, but in Japan, South Korea, and Singapore. Athletes are

[16] See Elizabeth C. Economy, *supra* note 5. Recently, China has moved to incorporate at least some consideration of environmental parameters. Charles R. McElwee II, *Who's Cleaning Up This Mess?*, CHINA BUSINESS REVIEW , January–February 2008.

[17] Beijing 2008, Green Olympics, http://en.beijing2008.cn/12/12/greenolympics.shtml.

[18] U.N. Environment Programme, Beijing 2008 Olympic Games—An Environmental Review, http://www.unep.org/Documents.Multilingual/Default.asp?DocumentID=519&ArticleID=5687&l=en. *See also Hazy Outlook for Games, supra* note 20.

also testing their ability to train with face masks in anticipation of the Beijing air quality.

In its own way, the 2008 Beijing Olympics demonstrates both everything China is doing well to provide a healthier environment for its residents and the challenges that lie ahead.

First, the Olympics demonstrate China's world-class sophistication and ability to understand, communicate, and address environmental issues and challenges. Since 2005, China has identified scores of environmental challenges confronting the 2008 Olympics and has devoted significant resources toward organizing solutions and communicating the results. This demonstrates a capacity and ability among China's leaders, scientists, and industries to understand the most complex environmental issues and develop solutions. In other words, the financial and technical resources needed to promote a better environment seem to be available.

Second, the 2008 Olympics demonstrates the government's flexibility in prioritizing environmental concerns and targeting solutions toward those concerns. In this case, China prioritized a better environment for Beijing in time for the events. In many (but not all) ways it appears to have realized that goal and in other ways it has demonstrated the significant creativity and resources China can put toward addressing a problem when it wants to. However, questions that must be considered after August include the extent to which China merely transported environmental concerns from one area to another, the extent to which this Olympic priority was at the expense of other existing environmental concerns, and the extent to which the lessons learned in Beijing will be applied elsewhere in China.

Third, critical to convincing the world of a message is the assurance that the message is authentic and that the public trusts it. In this way, China arguably has made less progress. The plethora of numbers, criteria, and accomplishments cited by the government frequently come without the transparency we would expect and which are critical to other environmental law frameworks. This in turn can raise doubts about authenticity. For example, while China earlier this year reported new statistics touting dramatically improved air quality in Beijing, one observer discovered that in fact some monitoring stations had been moved from inside the city core to less polluted areas.[19] On the other hand, there are some positive trends. When I was in Beijing, it so happened that the government published in the newspaper the text of a proposed water law, and solicited views on the law. But even with a potentially encouraging trend of promoting increased public participation into environmental regulation, the pace must improve for the public to have meaningful input.

Finally, perhaps the most significant contribution of the Green Olympics will be not any measurable environmental benefit, but a possible awakening to a new approach toward addressing both the economy and the environment. While the Olympics demonstrate that China can address a specific problem by prioritizing resources toward specific solutions, what is more sorely needed are approaches on a national scale. This will require a system of cooperative federalism that encourages local governments to realize and achieve the goals of a clean environment for the nation. While the American system of cooperative federalism admittedly does not translate in China, the government can emulate such a scheme by holding provincial and local officials accountable for environmental protection and results in addition to pure GDP. We may begin to see improvements along these lines in the coming months, if predictions about elevation of China's environmental agency stature and role are borne out and accompanied by improved institutional relationships and legal authorities.

Clearly, the Olympics have brought environmental improvements to the residents of Beijing. What the 2008 Olympics hopefully will bring to all China is an environmental awakening that it can realize a better environment and economic prosperity as mutually achievable—not exclusive—goals.

Thank you, Mr. Chairman, and members of the Commission. I would be happy to answer any questions you may have.

PREPARED STATEMENT OF SHARON HOM

FEBRUARY 27, 2008

Mr. Chairman, members of the Commission, on behalf of Human Rights in China (HRIC), thank you for the opportunity to make this statement. It is also an honor

---

[19] Stephen Q. Andrews, *Beijing's Sky Blues,* WALL STREET JOURNAL, Jan. 9, 2008.

to testify today alongside of the distinguished experts and human rights colleagues on this panel.

HRIC is an international, Chinese, non-governmental organization founded by Chinese students and scholars in March 1989. Our mission is to promote international human rights and advance the institutional protection of these rights in the People's Republic of China (China), and to provide concrete support and solidarity to human rights defenders. Through our Incorporating Responsibility 2008 Campaign, HRIC focuses on individual case advocacy, monitoring human rights progress in China, and promoting compliance with Beijing's Olympic Promises and other international human rights obligations in the lead-up to and beyond the 2008 Olympic Games.

With only about five months left until the opening of the 2008 Olympic Games, we appreciate the Commission's timely attention to the impact of the Olympics on human rights and the rule of law. As documented by the media, NGOs, United Nations, and government reports, including the Commission's 2007 Annual Report, crackdowns on human rights defenders in China have been increasing in the run-up to the Olympics. We welcomed the Commission's 2007 Annual Report, which not only called for an end to the harassment of Hu Jia and other activists, but also examined important issues regarding state secrets, civil society, petitioners, and ethnic minorities.

THE FALLACY OF "WITH US OR AGAINST US" OLYMPIC RHETORIC

One of the challenges to the advancement of human rights is the hostility of the Chinese authorities to any international or domestic human rights-related criticism, especially criticism tied to the Olympics. Chinese authorities have characterized any questioning of government policies in the lead-up to the Olympics as an attack on China itself. This intolerance for criticism, nationalism, and conflating of "China" with the Chinese government, was most recently exhibited in the response to Steven Spielberg's decision to withdraw from serving as artistic director of the opening and closing Olympic ceremonies. Chinese authorities first expressed regret, then slammed Mr. Spielberg. A government ready to host a major international event, a mature government that respects the rule of law, could have demonstrated a higher tolerance for thoughtful, critical and difficult individual decisions of the conscience. Instead, state-run media dismissed Mr. Spielberg as naïve and foolish.

This "with us or against us" mentality surrounding the Olympics fails to account for the legitimate concerns of domestic and international actors about the long-term impact of the Olympics, on both China's own people and the international community. Already we have seen that instead of serving as a catalyst for positive change, the Olympic preparations have been marked by or accompanied by crackdowns on dissent, massive displacements of residents,[1] and strain on already stretched environmental resources,[2] in order for China to put on its "best face" for the outside world.

CHINA'S OLYMPIC AND HUMAN RIGHTS OBLIGATIONS

By hosting the Games, Beijing is obligated to honor the commitments it made in the bidding process, which influenced the International Olympic Committee's (IOC) selection of the 2008 host city, and Beijing's own Olympic Promises.[3] During its 2001 bid for the Games, Beijing promised "complete freedom" for the media,[4] and IOC President Jacques Rogge stated in August 2001 that Beijing's host city contract included provisions guaranteeing media freedom for accredited press.[5] In March 2002, after the Games were awarded to Beijing, the Beijing Organizing Committee for the Olympic Games (BOCOG) released a Beijing Olympic Action Plan laying out the overall guidelines and plans for the preparation of the Olympics, shaped by the idea of "New Beijing, Great Olympics," with an emphasis on "Green Olympics," "High-Tech Olympics," "Free and Open Olympics," and "People's Olympics" as the

[1] See Centre On Housing Rights and Evictions (COHRE)'s report, "Fair Play for Housing Rights: Mega-Events, Olympic Games and Housing Rights", June 2007, http://www.cohre.org/store/attachments/COHRE%27s%20Olympics%20Report.pdf.

[2] See Chris Buckley, "Beijing Olympic Water Scheme Drains Parched Farmers," Environmental News Network, January 23, 2008, http://www.enn.com/wildlife/article/29488.

[3] See Sharon Hom, "The Promise of a 'People's Olympics,'" in *China's Great Leap: The Beijing Games and Olympian Human Rights Challenges,* ed. Minky Worden (Seven Stories Press, forthcoming May 2008).

[4] "Beijing Awaits Olympic Verdict", BBC, July 12, 2001, http://news.bbc.co.uk/sport2/hi/in_depth/2001/olympic_votes/1434964.stm.

[5] "Rogge: IOC Will Stick to Sports, Not Politics," Associated Press, August 27, 2001.

key to successful Games.[6] The 2002 Olympic Action Plan includes specific standards, such as technical environmental standards, to which Beijing would hold itself accountable in governance, construction of venues, and increasing social and economic development.[7]

As presented in the Action Plan, Beijing made the following Olympic Promises:

Green Olympics. "By 2008, we will achieve the goal of building the capital into an ecological city that features green hills, clear water, grass-covered ground, and blue sky."

High-Tech Olympics. "We will make all-out efforts to guarantee the security during the Olympic Games on the basis of a sound social order, reliable public transport and fire fighting systems, safe medical and health structures, and well planned supporting measures."

Free and Open Olympics. "In the preparation for the Games, we will be open in every aspect to the rest of the country and the whole world. We will draw on the successful experience of others and follow the international standards and criteria."

People's Olympics. "The Olympic Games will give an impetus to economic development and urban construction and management, and bring about increasing benefits for the people. We will make the preparations for the Olympic Games a process of substantially improving the people's living standard, both materially and culturally."

The Olympic Games is an event grounded in human dignity and the spirit of international cooperation of the Olympics movement. Liu Jianchao of the Ministry of Foreign Affairs has himself stated, "The Chinese Government will always be dedicated to improving and protecting human rights, be it prior to, or in the midst of or beyond the Beijing Olympics."[8] Indeed, we are all on the same page: the Olympics are China's opportunity to demonstrate to the world it is a responsible international citizen, one that lives up to its commitments, prior to, in the midst of, or beyond the Olympics.

The obligations of a country in hosting the Olympic Games, a major international event, are also part of and related to a country's overall international legal obligations, including human rights. As China's role in the international community expands and deepens, these international commitments are all inextricably linked. The link between human rights, democracy, and the Olympics was also made by Chinese officials during China's bid to host the 2008 Games and is reflected in the actual host city promises made. It is only by honoring these commitments that the Chinese authorities can host a truly successful Olympics, an event with a positive impact on China's people and the international community.

Additionally, China's actions in hosting the Olympics must be consistent with Chinese domestic law, including, for example, Article 35 of the Chinese Constitution, which protects "freedom of speech, of the press, of assembly, of association, of procession and of demonstration," and other constitutional provisions that protect freedom of privacy of correspondence (article 40) and the right to criticize the government (article 41).[9]

THE CRITICAL ROLE OF THE RULE OF LAW

Progress in building a rule of law is reflected in key benchmarks, including an independent judiciary and legal profession. China's criminal lawyers, however, face a number of impediments to providing an adequate defense: constraints on meeting with their clients, constraints on access to evidence, and in sensitive cases, lawyers themselves are sometimes harassed or intimidated. Over the past few years, there have been numerous cases of lawyers and legal advisors being intimidated and even beaten by the authorities or with official complicity. Rights-defense lawyers have been the target of varying levels of surveillance and harassment because of their

---

[6] Beijing Organizing Committee of the Olympic Games (BOCOG), Beijing Olympic Action Plan, March 2002. www.usembassy-china.org.cn/fcs/pdf/boap.doc

[7] Beijing Organizing Committee of the Olympic Games (BOCOG), Beijing Olympic Action Plan, March 2002. www.usembassy-china.org.cn/fcs/pdf/boap.doc

[8] "Foreign Ministry Spokesman Liu Jianchao's Regular Press Conference on February 21, 2008," February 22, 2008, http://www.chinaembassy-canada.org/eng/xwfw/s2510/2511/t409230.htm.

[9] However, the right to freedom of expression is constrained in China through the criminal and state secrets legal framework, and supported by broader police and social controls as well as sophisticated technology censorship and surveillance tools. HRIC and other groups have documented the use of state secrets crimes against lawyers, journalists, Internet activists and other human rights defenders as a means of controlling dissent. See Human Rights in China, *State Secrets: China's Legal Labyrinth,* June 12, 2007, http://hrichina.org/public/contents/41421.

work.[10] This lack of independent rule of law has implications in the realms of security (particularly post-Olympic use of sophisticated Olympic event surveillance equipment), media freedom, the development of civil society, and protection of human rights as a whole.

At the same time, there has been progress toward rebuilding the legal system in China in the last three decades, including legislation, training of legal personnel, and development of legal and administrative institutions and processes. Foreign actors such as foundations, governments, and academic institutions have supported exchanges and capacity-building initiatives. Substantive legislative initiatives to date have focused on economic law, civil law and other regulatory areas necessary to promote market reforms, along with administrative law and administrative procedure law.[11] Building a rule of law is a complex challenge, and China has been making encouraging strides in this respect, particularly with its enactment of the new Labor Contract Law[12] and revisions to the Lawyers' Law.[13]

The rule of law going forward must also be built on accountability and effective responses to the justice claims for past abuses. Today, at the request of the Tiananmen Mothers, a group within China comprised of family members of victims of the June 4, 1989 crackdown, HRIC is releasing the Tiananmen Mothers' letter calling for justice in the run-up to the Olympics. The open letter demonstrates the urgently-felt need of China's own people for rule of law. (Included as an addendum to this statement is the open letter, "An Appeal from the Tiananmen Mothers to the Government: Set a Timetable for Dialogue on the June Fourth Massacre.")

These brave individuals make clear in their letter that "the disastrous aftermath of that brutal massacre, one of the greatest tragedies of our times, even after 18 years, is still unresolved. The wounds deep in the heart of the people are not yet healed. Because of this, the current political and societal landscape continues to deteriorate into disorder and imbalance. This proves that June Fourth, this bloody page in history, has yet to be turned, and remains a 'knot' deep inside the people's heart. . . . The proper settlement of the 'June Fourth' question would represent not only a conclusion, but also a new beginning." The letter calls on the Chinese authorities to use legal means to investigate the tragedy and bring justice to the victims, so that China's society can heal and move forward in an open democratic way. The Tiananmen Mothers clearly link these challenges to the Olympics, asking, when the government has "repeatedly refused dialogue with the victims' family members . . . How can [it] face the whole world? Is it really possible that, as the host of the 2008 Olympic Games, the government can be at ease allowing athletes from all over the world to tread on this piece of blood-stained soil and participate in the Olympics?"

MAKING THE IMPACT OF THE OLYMPICS A POSITIVE ONE

The IOC's selection of Beijing as host of the 2008 Olympic Games is an incredible honor for the people of China, an honor that brings with it the potential for long-lasting, positive impact on the lives of individuals. HRIC is not calling for a boycott, and believes the hosting of the Games still presents an opportunity—and responsibility—to impact human rights and advance rule of law in China. It is up to each of the different actors and sectors[14]—governments, athletes, sponsors, tourists, businesses, corporate sponsors, academic exchange programs—to support the calls for reform coming from within China, and assess their roles and interactions with

---

[10] For more information, see HRIC's "About the Issue: Olympics and the Rule of Law," http://www.ir2008.org/02/issue.php.

[11] For more, see Sharon Hom, "Circling Towards Law," http://hrichina.org/public/PDFs/CRF.2.2007/CRF-2007-2_Circling.pdf.

[12] Labor Contract Law of the People's Republic of China, issued at the 28th Session of the Standing Committee of the 10th National People's Congress, June 29, 2007 and effective Jan. 1, 2008.

[13] Law of the People's Republic of China on Lawyers (2007 Revision), revised by the 30th Session of the 10th Standing Committee of NPC, October 28, 2007, to be enforced on June 1, 2008 (hereinafter as 2007 Lawyers Law). The Chinese text is available at: http://www.gov.cn/jrzg/2007-10/28/content_788495.htm.

[14] The projected attendance for the Olympics is staggering, and includes the following: 20,000–30,000 journalists; 10,500 athletes; 500,000–550,000 foreign visitors; over 2,000,000 domestic visitors; 70,000 volunteers working at the Olympics; and 30,000 volunteers for the Paralympics. See "Factbox: Olympics—Beijing By the Numbers," Reuters, August 7, 2007, http://www.reuters.com/article/latestCrisis/idUSSP176476; Beijing Organizing Committee of the Olympic Games, "Beijing 2008: Volunteer Recruitment Goes International," http://en.beijing2008.cn/68/95/article214029568.shtml; "Beijing Holds Grand Olympic Hopes," Associated Press (via CNN), August 11, 2007, http://edition.cnn.com/2007/WORLD/asiapcf/08/05/china.olympics.ap/index.html; "Computerized Polyglots to Serve Beijing Olympics," People's Daily, September 11, 2007, http://english.peopledaily.com.cn/90001/90781/90879/6260185.html.

China. Each actor can use different opportunities to advance the rule of law, a successful Olympics, and the human rights of China's people. It is clear that we can no longer continue "business as usual."

The international community needs to first get behind the hype and the spin to find accurate information about what's really going on in China. We would like to close with some recommendations and suggestions for the Commission:

- Raise individual cases in U.S. high-level visits and other fora with Chinese authorities: Such action sends a clear message of support and concern for human rights. Secretary Rice's recently reported engagement with Beijing on human rights issues is a good example. We urge the Commission members to support the cases of the individuals featured in HRIC's Incorporating Responsibility 2008 Campaign.[15] These 12 human rights defenders, including Shi Tao, Chen Guangcheng, and other individuals imprisoned for rights-related work, collectively represent the range of human rights issues that are of serious concern in China today.

- Particular attention should also be paid to cases that involve individuals who have raised Olympics-related criticisms, including:

Hu Jia: HIV/AIDS activist Hu Jia posted an article on the real situation of China in the lead-up to the Olympics.[16] He was detained on December 27, 2007, on charges of "inciting subversion of state power." He is currently being held at Beijing Municipal Detention Centre and has been denied release on bail pending investigation for reportedly being a danger to society.

Gao Zhisheng: In September 2007, Gao Zhisheng wrote a 16-page open letter to the U.S. Congress detailing the human rights situation and anti-Olympics sentiment in China, and called for a boycott of the Olympics, alleging that the CCP was using the Games as a tool to assume legitimacy.[17] Gao was detained in mid-September 2007; his current situation is unclear.

Yang Chunlin: Yang Chunlin is a Heilongjiang land rights activist detained in July 2007 after organizing the "We Want Human Rights, Not the Olympics" (also known as "Human Rights Over the Olympics") petition that gained over 10,000 signatures. He was formally arrested in August 2007 and charged with incitement to subvert state power.[18] In February 2008, Yang's trial opened in the city of Jiamusi, but no verdict has yet been reached. Yang's arrest and trial are notable because the case is one of the first that openly ties opposition to the Beijing Olympics to allegations of subversion.[19]

Ye Guozhu: Ye Guozhu is a 52-year-old housing advocate and a Beijing resident, who was evicted from his home in May 2003 to make way for Olympic construction. In August 2004, Ye applied for permission to organize a demonstration of 10,000 against forced Olympic evictions. After the application, he was detained on August 28, 2004, on suspicion of "disturbing social order" and other public order offenses. He was formally arrested on September 15, 2004, after two weeks of detention.[20] In December 2004, Ye was sentenced to four years in prison by the Dongcheng city court for "picking a quarrel and making trouble."[21] He is due for release in mid-July 2008.

Wang Dejia: Wang wrote articles criticizing Beijing for human rights abuses, and stated that China's central government was ignoring the needs of common people in the lead-up to the Olympics and was more concerned about cracking down on dissidents and building new venues. Wang was detained on December 14, 2007, on a charge of "subverting state authority."[22]

---

[15] The campaign website is located at http://www.ir2008.org/.

[16] See Teng Biao and Hu Jia, "The Real Situation in Pre-Olympics China," available at http://hrichina.org/public/PDFs/CRF.4.2007/CRF-2007-4_Situation.pdf.

[17] "China Dissident Urges Boycott of Olympics," The Washington Times, September 21, 2007, http://www.washingtontimes.com/apps/pbcs.dll/article?AID=/20070921/NATION/109210069/1002/NATION&template=nextpage.

[18] "Chinese Land Rights Activist Who Opposed Olympics Will Go On Trial Next Week, Lawyer Says," Associated Press (via International Herald Tribune), February 15, 2008, http://www.iht.com/articles/ap/2008/02/15/news/China-Activist.php.

[19] "China Tries Land Activist Who Opposed Olympics," Radio Free Asia, February 19, 2008, http://www.rfa.org/english/news/2008/02/19/china_olympics/.

[20] "'Key Protester' for 'Troublemaking' Arrested in China," Kyodo News, September 28, 2004.

[21] "Chinese Activist Gets Four Years in Jail for Planning Demonstration," Agence-France Presse, December 17, 2004.

[22] Anita Chang, "Chinese activist held for subversion," AP, December 19, 2007, http://news.yahoo.com/s/ap/20071219/ap_on_re_as/china_dissident_detained_1;_ylt=Am75FBgAk5.2qzyFGJnC85NPzWQA.

• Monitor censorship and surveillance: We are pleased to see the U.S. National Olympic Committee has not issued any orders to U.S. athletes limiting their speech while in China, and we hope U.S. dialogue with China will serve as one way to engage on human rights issues and support freedom of expression. Regarding surveillance, the Chinese government is responsible for providing appropriate security during the Olympics and beyond. We urge the Commission members to monitor two areas of concern: first, the appropriate balancing of security and protections for human rights; and second, the post-Olympic uses of the advanced security technology being developed and implemented for the Olympics. This technology will be in place long after the Games are over and the international media have packed up, and further consideration is required regarding its impact on human rights.[23]

• Review of dual-use export control regulations by the Commerce Department: We understand the Commerce Department is currently revisiting U.S.-China dual-use export control regulations, specifying what security equipment American companies can sell to China. In response to rapid advances in surveillance technology and the increasing involvement of American companies in the Chinese market, the Commerce Department was reported as singling out biometric technology—face-recognition software—which Chinese security agencies could misuse against rights defenders and others. Through appropriate channels with Commerce, Commission members should raise human rights concerns, including concerns regarding corporations that sell equipment directly to the Chinese police.

• Finally, HRIC strongly urges the Commission members to publicly express their support for the Tiananmen Mothers, and other domestic rights defenders. Despite the dismissals of June Fourth as belonging to the past by IOC President Jacques Rogge and others, the June Fourth crackdown still plays a defining role in the lives of China's people today.

Respected members of the international community emerge not through elaborately orchestrated spectacles, expensive stadiums, mascots or international fanfare—but by respecting human rights at home and abroad. HRIC hopes the Chinese government will take the opportunity of the Olympic Games, as the whole world is watching, to do just that.

Thank you and I look forward to your questions.

––––––––

PREPARED STATEMENT OF ROBERT DIETZ

FEBRUARY 27, 2008

Dear Chairman and distinguished members of the Congressional-Executive Commission on China:

Thank you for inviting the Committee to Protect Journalists to participate in the discussion of "The Impact of the 2008 Olympic Games on Human Rights and the Rule of Law in China." CPJ has been monitoring press freedom conditions in China and around the world for more than 25 years. The organization was founded in 1981 by a group of American journalists who believed that the strength and influence of the international media could be used to support journalists who are targeted because of their work. CPJ is independently funded by individuals, foundations and corporations, and accepts no government funds whatsoever.

Recognizing that with the advent of the 2008 Beijing Games we were presented with an opportunity to exert greater than usual influence around China's media policy, last year CPJ produced a report, "Falling Short: As the 2008 Olympics Approach, China Falters on Press Freedom," which we are in the process of revising for this year. Our intention was to speak to the more than 25,000 journalists expected to descend on China for the 2008 Summer Olympic Games. We wanted to give them practical advice on how to work as a journalist in China, as well as tell them of the conditions under which their Chinese colleagues are working.

That second point, conditions for Chinese journalists, is a critical one. We are concerned that when foreign news teams arriving in Beijing hire local Chinese assistants they will place demands on them that might put them in jeopardy. Reporters who ask their Chinese hires to arrange potentially dangerous meetings, say with activists, or to visit an AIDS village, or get advance information on potential demonstrations that the government will want to quash, might be putting their Chinese colleagues at risk. It is not inconceivable that they will be made to pay a price, if

––––––––

[23] See Keith Bradsher, "China Finds American Allies for Security," New York Times, December 28, 2007.

not during the Games, then after them, when the world's media attention has moved on.

Watching China make preparations for the Games, it is clear the government wants them to come off without a flaw. That preoccupation could lead to overly aggressive attempts to control the media, a pattern we believe we are already seeing. While those attempts will most likely be futile, past experience has shown that China tends to err on the side of heavy-handedness when it comes to media control and threats to China's image as a unified nation with little internal dissent. We are not as concerned about the threat that foreign journalists will face in China during the Games, but it seems that the Chinese journalists working with them as translators, fixers, and coordinators—many of whom will be enthusiastic young people with relatively little journalism experience—make up a high-risk group.

Just how high are the risks for Chinese journalists in China? It is a mixed picture. Here are the harshest facts first:

With less than one year to go before the 2008 Olympic Games, China is holding at least 25 reporters and editors behind bars because of their work. Most journalists are being held on vague security-related charges such as revealing state secrets or inciting subversion of state power. By hiding behind such broad accusations of threats to civil stability, China has been the world's leading jailer of journalists since 1999. That number of 25 behind bars is down from 29 last year.

Typical is the case of Shi Tao, whose mother has called on CPJ to pressure the international community to insist Chinese authorities to release her son ahead of the 2008 Olympic Games in Beijing. "My son is not guilty. You should keep up pressure on the Chinese government to release him," Gao Qinsheng said when she visited CPJ's office in June of last year. Shi is serving a 10-year prison term for the crime of "leaking state secrets abroad." He was jailed in 2004 for sending an e-mail describing Communist Party propaganda department orders to his newspaper Dangdai Shangbao (Contemporary Trade News). The information included orders to news editors on how to report the anniversary of the 1989 crackdown on Tiananmen Square demonstrators.

But there has been a thaw of sorts in recent weeks. Li Changqing and Yue Tianxiang were both released within the past two months because their sentences were due to expire. The Singapore Straits Times journalist Ching Cheong was released unexpectedly on February 7 after campaigns for his health, while Southern Metropolis News journalist Yu Huafeng was released on February 11 after his sentence was commuted through a lengthy appeal process. It is worth noting that all but one of these men was a fairly senior print journalist. And we believe the December 2006 release of a former Xinhua reporter, Gao Qinrong after serving eight years of a 12-year sentence falls into the same category. Senior journalists working in what are government-controlled publications seem to receive softer government treatment, possibly because their arrests and sentences were so egregious in the first place—if we dare to think that reduced time behind bars for simply having worked as a journalist can be classified as "softer treatment."

Are these recent releases an indicator of a change of heart on the part of the Chinese government? It is difficult to say, but my feeling is that it is most likely not, though China has used prisoner releases to ease international criticism in the past. And remember, on about the same day Ching Cheong was released and allowed to return to his family in Hong Kong, Lü Gengsong was sentenced to four years in prison on subversion charges by the Intermediate People's Court in the eastern Chinese city of Hangzhou, after his one-day, closed-door trial on January 22. Lü was sentenced for "inciting the subversion of state power." Lü is a strong populist who openly criticized corrupt officials,µand wrote several articles for overseas Web sites and reported on the trial of a human rights defender the day before he was arrested.

Mo Shaoping, a veteran Beijing-based lawyer who has represented many jailed journalists, told CPJ that he did not take the recent releases as encouraging signs. "There has been no reduction in cases where subversion charges are brought against people for articles they have written. If anything," Mr. Mo told us, "these cases have increased in the past one or two years."

CPJ's records show that three more jailed journalists are due to be released before or around the time the Games start on August 8.

• Hua Di is a Stanford University researcher and U.S. resident who was charged with revealing state secrets while visiting China in January 1998 after publishing articles about China's defense system in academic journals. We have been unable to confirm his whereabouts.

• Zhang Wei was arrested in July 2002 for illegally publishing underground newspapers that officials said "misled the public" in Chongqing, central China. He is due out in July.

- Fan Yingshang printed 60,000 copies of a magazine and was subsequently charged with profiteering in October 1995. Fan is due to be released sometime before October.

CPJ is calling on China to release these men immediately, and then begin a review of its media policies. It seems clear that China's leaders have grasped the importance of the open flow of information to a modern economy. Jailing journalists goes back to an era when the government thought it could control every aspect of a Chinese citizen's life. It long ago relinquished that notion, but it persists in jailing journalists as if China were still at the height of the Cultural Revolution.

An important fact to remember is that more than half of the journalists behind bars in China are there for Internet-related activities. But despite having the world's greatest Internet censorship apparatus, the government seems unable to fully stem the flow of frank discussion and open criticism that ricochets across China from e-mail, blogs, foreign and domestic Web sites, message bulletin boards, instant messaging and telephone texting. The highly vaunted Great Firewall of China is under constant pressure, and is turning more into an increasingly leaky dike holding back a rising digital flood of information with constantly updated technology, some of it supplied by United States companies. The government is struggling to stay on top of the growth of the Internet.

And the Internet is not the only place where China's attempts to control the flow of information are not meeting with success.

The number of journalists jailed in China does not tell the whole story. The overwhelmingly vast majority of journalists in China are not in jail. Many reporters in the country's ever-more commercialized media are pursuing news stories and readers with energy and enthusiasm, while their editors fully understand how far they can push the limits of a story. To rein in that energy, the government propaganda machine hands down a daily stream of directives covering issues that range from the most sensitive—how to handle the annual commemoration of the 1989 Tiananmen demonstrations, or a toxic chemical spill into a river, say—to the most mundane tabloid-level stories. Reporters and editors know they are being watched and a running tally of their missteps is kept. Too many errors could mean a demotion or reassignment to a less prestigious publication, far away from home. Successful journalists and editors pick their battles carefully, knowing their readers and viewers increasingly expect reliable and accurate reporting. Many others simply resign themselves to the restrictions, write the party line, and take home their paycheck.

It is interesting to note the directives from the Central Propaganda Department are no longer always delivered by e-mail anymore, according to journalists we have spoken with in Hong Kong earlier this month. Increasingly, directives are given by telephone, so that there is no electronic trail of the department's messages. We have been told that the method changed after our use of some of those messages appeared in "Falling Short," CPJ's report on the Olympics, which I mentioned at the beginning of these remarks.

The method of transmission of censorship directives is one change in China's well-oiled control system, and not necessarily one for the better. And it is not the sort of change we were assured we would see after Beijing was awarded the 2008 Olympic Games. The International Olympic Committee and the government assured skeptics that the influx of Olympic ideals would wean the government from its obsession with regulating the flow of information.

That scenario never came to pass and doesn't look likely to, though some restrictions on foreign journalists were lifted in January 2007. Under the new rules foreigners are allowed unrestricted travel and are free to ask questions of anyone willing to talk to them—rules that were largely ignored anyway. Government officials have talked about the possibility that those restrictions will be fully lifted sometime soon, never to return—though it should be noted that travel to Tibet and the Xinjiang Autonomous Region are still forbidden.

Foreign journalists in China do report fewer hassles and restrictions since the new regulations were handed down, although many local officials and powerful businessmen have yet to get the message at the grassroots level. There continue to be disturbing reports of the harassment of Chinese citizens who have given interviews to foreign reporters. And most foreign journalists still operate under the assumption that their phones are tapped and e-mail monitored.

For Chinese journalists things have gotten worse. Many of them have told CPJ that while they wish they had the freedoms their foreign colleagues now have, they would be reluctant to exercise them anyway. They fear retribution once the spotlight of the Games has moved on and the country reverts to business as usual.

Still, the government is clearly fighting a rear guard action in trying to control the flow of information. Increasingly media—particularly print media—push those limits. Internet-based citizen journalists abound and bona fide press-card holders regularly put their stories online if they can't convince their papers to run with them. The journalism instinct is alive and well in China. It is the government that is still stuck in its Mao-era approach, trying to cope with the demands of increasingly sophisticated journalists and their readers and viewers.

This is the atmosphere into which some 20,000 to 30,000 foreign journalists and technicians will find themselves in August 2008. Given that it does not look like China will soften its stance any more, and that it has even come down harder on its own journalists in recent months, what can be done?

- CPJ and other groups have not had any apparent success in dealing with the International Olympic Committee around these issues. We are calling on governments, particularly our own, and the Games' corporate sponsors to press the International Olympic Committee to insist that the Chinese government fully meet its promises of press freedom for the 2008 Games. And we want to ensure that freedom is extended to Chinese journalists, though I suspect our Chinese colleagues would be wary of immediately taking advantage of those freedoms.
- We ask everyone to continue to call on China to meet the pledge made to the IOC in 2001 when it was awarded the Games to remove media restrictions. In particular, eliminate restrictions on local journalists, who continue to face the same severe constraints they did before China was awarded the Games in 2001.
- We do not think it is unrealistic to call on China to release all the journalists currently imprisoned for their work. For them to be in jail when the Games begin on August 8, 2008, would make a travesty of China's pledge of greater press freedom and the IOC's acceptance of that pledge.
- In the broadest sense, China should stop censoring news and dismantle the archaic system of media control that has evolved over several decades. Halt Internet censorship and monitoring activities and let information flow freely on every digital platform.
- Narrow the use of state secret and national security laws, bringing them into compliance with the Johannesburg Principles on National Security, Freedom of Expression, and Access to Information. These principles, endorsed by the U.N. special rapporteur on freedom of opinion and expression, allow restrictions only in cases of legitimate national security.
- Ratify the International Covenant on Civil and Political Rights, which China signed in 1998. Article 19 of the Covenant states: "Everyone shall have the right to freedom of expression; this right shall include freedom to seek, receive, and impart information and ideas of all kinds, regardless of frontiers, either orally, in writing or in print, in the form of art, or through any other media of his choice."
- As a member of the United Nations, honor Article 19 of the Universal Declaration of Human Rights, which states: "Everyone has the right to freedom of opinion and expression; this right includes freedom to hold opinions without interference and to seek, receive, and impart information and ideas through any media and regardless of frontiers."

And, perhaps most important, we are calling on the international media organizations that will be in China to do two things and do them with the same dedication and energy they will use to cover the Games:

- Use all means to insist that China honor its media pledges to the IOC and extend to Chinese journalists the same freedoms that visiting journalists enjoy.
- For the safety and well-being of our Chinese colleagues, take extra steps to ensure that all employees covering the games, either on the ground in China or on editorial desks at home offices, to be aware of the restrictions and threats that their Chinese colleagues face. Chinese journalists are not allowed to operate under the same rules that foreign journalists take for granted. To forget that reality can endanger their freedom.

I thank the Commission for the opportunity it has granted CPJ to outline these issues. Along with this testimony, we have submitted a copy of our report, "Falling Short," for your reference.

PREPARED STATEMENT OF SOPHIE RICHARDSON

FEBRUARY 27, 2008

Chairman Levin, Co-Chairman Dorgan, and other Distinguished Members of the Commission,

Human Rights Watch first wishes to thank the CECC for convening this timely hearing. It is a privilege to participate along with such distinguished panelists.

There are three key questions before us today. The first is whether the human rights situation in advance of the 2008 Beijing Games is improving, as the Chinese government has repeatedly insisted it would. We regretfully submit that it is not. Over the past year, we have continued to document not only chronic human rights abuses inside China, such as restrictions on basic freedoms of speech, assembly, and political participation, but also abuses that are taking place specifically as a result of China's hosting the 2008 Summer Games. Those include an increasing use of house arrest and charges of "inciting subversion" as means of silencing dissent, on-going harassment of foreign journalists despite new regulations protecting them, and abuses of migrant construction workers without whose labors Beijing's gleaming new skyline would not exist. More detail about these and other abuses are included in our written testimony.

The second key question is whether this negative impact will be a lasting one. Human Rights Watch believes that these abuses constitute a failure of the Chinese government to fulfill its own voluntarily made promises to improve rights in order to win the bid to host the Olympics. These were promises made to the international community, to the International Olympic Committee, and, indeed, to the Chinese people. It is clear that the Chinese government has no intention of following through on these commitments, and unless significant pressure is brought to bear to make it do so, we fear the negative impact will not only be very difficult to reverse in the future, but will also mean that in effect the international community has tacitly endorsed the repression necessary to engineer a vision of a modern, cosmopolitan China.

The third question, therefore, is what we can do to alter the current situation to ensure a better outcome. The administration and State Department assure us that they are constantly raising these concerns, and while we do not doubt their efforts, we question the efficacy of "quiet diplomacy" in the absence of more public measures—after all, the decreasing volume of American criticism of China's rights record over the past decade is in part to blame for the current situation, and President Bush and Secretary Rice managed over the course of just a few days last week to contradict one another as to whether the United States feels it is appropriate to raise rights issues in the context of the Olympics. The Chinese government desperately wants a positive international assessment of its country during this time of unprecedented scrutiny; we believe that if pressed, they will make progress in order to get such reviews, particularly from the United States.

To that end, Human Rights Watch respectfully urges that:

1. All members of Congress and senior administration officials who visit China in the coming months speak publicly about these abuses, and, when security for all involved can be ensured, visit those under house or actual arrest for challenging the Chinese government's rights abuses.

2. The members of this Commission request public assurances from US-based Olympic sponsors that their business practices in China do not contribute to rights abuses.

3. That the Administration be asked to articulate how it will respond to rights abuses in the coming months, including how it is prepared to assist American journalists who are intimidated, harassed, or detained while trying to do their jobs.

4. That the Administration explain what specific rights-promoting activities the President will engage in while in Beijing to demonstrate that his rhetorical commitments be made real. These could include making himself available for on-line discussions to underscore the importance of internet freedom, visiting unregistered churches to emphasize the right to practice religion freely, or speaking publicly about the constraints under which Chinese journalists are forced to operate.

5. And, if the current crackdown shows no sign of abating in the coming months, ask the Administration to publicly reconsider whether it is still appropriate for the President to attend the opening or closing ceremonies.

If steps like these are not taken—and taken soon—the U.S. government runs the risk of giving an imprimatur of approval to the Chinese government's rights record.

Thank you for the opportunity to participate and for the Commission's ongoing commitment to human rights issues.

BACKGROUND ON HUMAN RIGHTS ABUSES IN ADVANCE OF THE 2008 BEIJING OLYMPICS

Despite China's official assurances that hosting the 2008 Olympic Games will help to strengthen the development of human rights in the country, the Chinese government continues to deny or restrict its citizens' fundamental rights, including freedom of expression, freedom of association, and freedom of religion.

The government's extensive police and state security apparatus continues to impose multiple layers of controls on civil society activists, critics, and protesters. Those layers include professional and administrative measures, limitations on foreign travel and domestic movement, monitoring (covert or overt) of internet and phone communications, abduction and confinement incommunicado, and unofficial house arrests. A variety of vaguely defined crimes including "inciting subversion," "leaking state secrets," and "disrupting social order" provide the government with wide legal remit to stifle critics.

HUMAN RIGHTS AND THE 2008 OLYMPICS

Despite temporary regulations in effect from January 1, 2007, to October 17, 2008, that give correspondents freedom to interview anyone who consents, foreign journalists continue to be harassed, detained, and intimidated by government and police officials. The temporary regulations do not extend to Chinese journalists or foreign correspondents' Chinese assistants, researchers, and sources, who continue to risk reprisals for violating government directives on taboo reporting topics.

Official efforts to rid Beijing of undesirables ahead of the Olympics have accelerated the eviction of petitioners—citizens from the countryside who come to the capital seeking redress for grievances ranging from illegal land seizures to official corruption. In September–October the Beijing municipal government demolished a settlement in Fengtai district that housed up to 4,000 petitioners.

The countdown to the Olympics has also sparked a construction boom. An estimated one million migrant construction workers are integral to this effort, yet their labor conditions are harsh and unsafe, and workers are often unable to access public services. When a subway tunnel under construction collapsed in March, trapping six workers, the first step the employer took was to prevent workers from reporting the accident by confiscating their mobile phones.

FREEDOM OF EXPRESSION

In 2007 the Chinese government stepped up its efforts to control increasingly vibrant print and online forms of expression, and sanctioned individuals, journalists, and editors for failing to conform to highly restrictive but inconsistently implemented laws and regulations.

China's system of internet censorship and surveillance is the most advanced in the world. Filtering, blocking, and monitoring technologies are built into all layers of China's internet infrastructure. Tens of thousands of police remotely monitor internet use around the clock. The elaborate system of censorship is aided by extensive corporate and private sector cooperation—including by some of the world's major international technology and internet companies such as Google, Yahoo, and Microsoft. Writers, editors, bloggers, webmasters, and journalists risk punishments ranging from immediate dismissal to prosecution and lengthy jail terms for sending news outside China or posting articles critical of the political system. For example, Zhang Jianhong, former editor-in-chief of the Aegean Sea website, was sentenced to six years' imprisonment on March 19 for "inciting subversion."

The countdown to the Beijing Olympics has seen the threshold lowered for internet content considered "sensitive" by China's censors and prompted closure of access to thousands of websites in 2007, including popular international sites such as Wikipedia and Flickr. The government has expanded its traditional criteria for internet censorship from topics including references to the 1989 Tiananmen Massacre, the outlawed Falungong "evil cult," and content perceived as sympathetic to "separatist" elements in Tibet, Xinjiang, and Taiwan, to include "unauthorized" coverage of everything from natural disasters to corruption scandals that might embarrass the Communist Party of China (CPC). By official estimate the government shut down more than 18,000 individual blogs and websites since April 2007, and in August censors widened their focus to include shutting down numerous internet data centers. Official measures to filter or remove "sensitive" content from domestic websites sharply accelerated in the run up to the 17th CPC Congress in October.

Chinese journalists continue to risk severe repercussions for pursuing stories that touch on officially taboo subjects or threaten powerful private interests. Miao Wei, former executive editor of Sanlian Life Weekly, confirmed in April that he had been demoted in connection with a cover story on the aftermath of the Cultural Revolution (1966–1976). Lan Chengzhang, a reporter with China Trade News, was murdered in January while investigating an illegal coal mine in Datong, Shanxi province. In mid-August five journalists, including a reporter from the government mouthpiece People's Daily, were interviewing witnesses to the Fenghuang bridge collapse in Hunan province when plainclothes thugs interrupted the interviews and kicked and punched the journalists, who were then detained by police.

LEGAL REFORM

Legal reforms proceeded at a fast pace in 2007 in order to achieve the CPC's overriding goal of making the rule of law "the principal tool to govern the country." New legislation was adopted on a wide range of issues such as property rights, labor contracts, administration of lawyers, access to public records, and the handling of emergencies. But the party's continued dominance over, and interference with, judicial institutions, as well as weak and inconsistent enforcement of judicial decisions,μmeans that overall the legal system remains vulnerable to arbitrary interference.

Ordinary citizens face immense obstacles to accessing justice, in particular over issues such as illegal land seizures, forced evictions, environmental pollution, unpaid wages, corruption, and abuse of power by local officials, a situation that fuels rising social unrest across the country. The authorities have stopped disclosing figures about the number of riots and demonstrations after they announced a decline from over 200 incidents per day in 2006, but large-scale incidents were reported in 2007 in almost all of China's 34 province-level administrative units. Several demonstrations involved tens of thousand of people, such as in Yongzhou (Hunan) in March 2007 and Xiamen (Fujian) in June. In speeches and articles top security officials acknowledged the heightening of social conflicts, but remained defiant toward greater independence of the judiciary, blaming "hostile" or "enemy forces" for trying to use the nation's legal system to undermine and westernize China. A string of lawyers defending human rights cases have been suspended or disbarred under a yearly licensing system that acts as a general deterrent to taking cases viewed as "sensitive" by the authorities.

The rights of criminal defendants continued to be sharply limited and violated by law enforcement agencies. Defense lawyers face chronic difficulties including accessing defendants in custody, consulting court documents, and producing exculpatory evidence before the court. Despite the reiteration by the Supreme People's Court in September that judges ought to "pay more attention to evidence and treat confessions with more skepticism," torture, especially at the pretrial stage, remains prevalent. The Public Security Bureau continues to make wide use, including for political and religious dissidents, of the Reeducation-Through-Labor system, which allows detention for up to four years for "minor offenders," without trial.

HUMAN RIGHTS DEFENDERS

Chinese human rights defenders, seizing on the official promise of lawful governance, are becoming more assertive and skillful at documenting abuses and mounting legal challenges. But the authorities, who have never tolerated independent human rights monitoring, have retaliated with harassment, unlawful detention, forced disappearances, and long prison sentences, often on trumped-up charges.

Authorities have targeted a small, loosely-organized network of lawyers, legal academics, rights activists, and journalists, known as the weiquan movement, which aims to pursue social justice and constitutional rights through litigation. The movement focuses on the protection of ordinary citizens over issues such as housing rights, land seizures, workers' rights, and police abuse. Yang Chunlin, a land rights activist arrested in July, was found guilty in February 2008 of "inciting subversion" for his role in organizing a petition titled "We want human rights, not the Olympics." Lu Gengsong, a former lecturer turned activist who documented illegal eviction cases and official collusion, was found guilty in February 2008 on charges of subverting state power. In August 2007 environmental activist Wu Lihong was sentenced to three years' imprisonment under ill-defined business fraud charges; his wife reported he had been tortured while held incommunicado. Yang Maodong, a Guangzhou-based land rights activist arrested in September 2006 and still awaiting trial, also reported that he had been repeatedly tortured in detention.

Defenders who document and report abuses against other activists are particularly vulnerable. In September lawyer Li Heping was abducted in broad daylight, held for six hours, severely beaten, and told he should leave Beijing. Li Jianqiang, a renowned human rights lawyer, was disbarred without reason. The human rights monitor Hu Jia has been maintained in house arrest in Beijing for the most part of the year out of any legal procedure. Yuan Weijing, the wife of the blind activist Chen Guangcheng who is currently serving a three-year sentence for exposing family planning abuses, was also prevented from traveling abroad to collect a human rights prize on his behalf.

LABOR RIGHTS

Chinese workers continue to be forbidden to form independent trade unions, as the government maintains that the party-controlled All-China Federation of Trade Unions (ACFTU) adequately protects workers' rights. This restriction on legally-sanctioned labor activism, coupled with increasingly tense labor disputes in which protesting workers have few realistic routes for redress, have contributed to increasing numbers of workers taking to the streets and to the courts to press claims about forced and uncompensated overtime, employer violations of minimum wage rules, unpaid pensions and wages, and dangerous and unhealthy working environments.

Workers who seek redress through strike action are often subject to attacks by plainclothes thugs who appear to operate at the behest of employers. In July a group of 200 thugs armed with spades, axes, and steel pipes attacked a group of workers in Heyuan (Guangdong), who were protesting over not having been paid for four months; they beat one worker to death.

Human Rights Watch will soon release a report detailing abuses of migrant construction workers in Beijing.

FREEDOM OF RELIGION

The Chinese government recognizes the right to believe, but limits worship to a state-controlled system of registered and controlled churches, congregations, mosques, monasteries, and temples.

The official registration process requires government vetting and ongoing scrutiny of religious publications, seminary applications, and religious personnel. The government also closely monitors the membership and financial records of religious institutions and the personnel they employ, and retains the right to approve or deny applications for any group activities by religious organizations. Those who fail to register are considered illegal and are liable for criminal prosecution, fines, and closure.

Reprisals against non-registered religious organizations have primarily focused on arrests of Protestants who attend "house churches," for Bible study meetings and training sessions. The majority of those arrested are rapidly released, some after paying fines, but leaders of such underground churches are sometimes held on fabricated charges including "illegal business practices." The freedom of belief of certain groups designated by the government as "evil cults," including Falungong, continues to be severely restricted.

———

PREPARED STATEMENT OF ROBIN MUNRO

FEBRUARY 27, 2008

Mr. Chairman, thank you for inviting me to testify at this important hearing. The focus of my comments today is on China's current labor rights situation, but I would like to broaden this theme to address the wider range of human and labor rights problems faced by ordinary, non-elite members of society—or what we at China Labour Bulletin sometimes call "human rights for the millions." Because time is short, I'm not going to say much about the Beijing Olympics themselves, but instead will simply offer a few broad-brushstroke thoughts and conclusions on the implications of the upcoming Games for the rights situation in China. I shall then fast-forward to the post-Olympics period and issues—or rather, try to review the basic underlying problems in society that are going on right now and which will still be there, virtually unchanged, after the Olympic athletes and visitors have all gone home.

The public notice for today's hearing poses the question of "whether the Olympics will bring lasting benefits to Chinese citizens," or, conversely, "have a negative impact on their human rights." With less than six months to go before the Games begin, I feel only one conclusion is possible here. Over the past year or so, the Games have led to a harsh and growing crackdown against the domestic civil rights movement, and to increasingly unrestrained rights violations by the government and security forces in general. Rights activists have been rounded up by the police and jailed, civil rights lawyers have been intimidated and punished, and even the wives of dissidents have been persecuted in an effort to ensure their silence as the

Olympic Games approach. As other speakers have noted, several rights activists are now facing criminal trials in China merely for calling on the government to give human rights a modicum of priority in the run-up to the all-important Games. In short, the official message being sent to China's citizens today is that any kind of public activity that in any way threatens to tarnish the authorities' image, or that introduces a negative note into the coming Olympics festivities, is de facto a crime. This official record makes a mockery of Beijing's pledges to the IOC and the world that holding the Olympic Games would advance the human rights cause in China. Clearly, Beijing 2008 is not going to be anything like Seoul in 1988.

Unfortunately, this outcome was largely to be expected. So much is riding on the forthcoming Games being a success, in terms both of the image the Chinese leadership wishes to project at the international level, and also of the message of rosy domestic contentment and rising popular prosperity that it wishes to impose on the Chinese people, that nothing is to be allowed to spoil the Olympics party. There is little the rest of the world can do about this, except to protest loudly and strongly as the crackdown continues. The one issue so far on which Games-related international pressure appears to have had a noticeably positive effect is the Darfur situation, via China's belated support for a U.N. peacekeeping force. But with Western governments no longer being willing to back up their words of censure with meaningful action or sanctions of any kind, and with China's economy now playing such a pivotal role on the world stage, Beijing clearly considers that it has little really to lose by toughing things out internationally while maintaining tight political control at home.

I should stress that the above remarks are not meant to suggest that Olympics-related pressure campaigns at this stage are pointless. Far from it: such campaigns are a vital means of ensuring that the Chinese authorities at least avoid the worst excesses of repression, in their zeal to present a smiling and united national face to the world this August. My point is simply that we should not hold any real hopes that the Games may somehow turn out to be a plus factor for the human rights or labor rights cause in China. It is conceivable that Beijing may produce a "trump card" on the eve of the Olympics—for example, by announcing ratification of the ICCPR, or by releasing one or more high-profile political prisoners—but that would serve mainly as a smokescreen to deflect international attention away from the continuing Games-related crackdown on civil liberties. Given the severity of the current clampdown on rights, such a gesture would be hollow and meaningless.

Nonetheless, because so many ordinary Chinese feel real pride at Beijing's hosting of the Games, I hope they will be a success. China is a great nation, and its people deserve their turn at the Olympics, even if the government does not. Also, if hosting the Games smoothly makes the Chinese leadership feel more secure domestically, that's probably a good thing: a more relaxed and confident government in Beijing is more likely to take steps, eventually, toward some degree of liberalization than a chronically scared and brittle one. The danger, however, is that the tight social and political controls set in place for the upcoming Olympics will—once the Games are over—simply become the "new normal" in China's internal security regime. If this happens, the Games will have set the clock back on human rights and civil liberties.

A SOCIALLY DIVIDED NATION—AND AN EMERGING CIVIL SOCIETY

The Chinese government nowadays strives to project the twin images of "the harmonious society" and (through the Olympics) of "one world, one dream." The reality, however, is that China today is far from being harmonious, and it embodies two very different worlds and dreams. On the one hand, there are those of the rising new elite, who enjoy unfettered access to all the best things in life; and on the other, those of the ordinary people, hundreds of millions of citizens who have no meaningful vote and whose main dream is somehow to make ends meet for the family until the next payday. In the government's view, however, if the desired "social harmony" cannot be achieved through consensus, then it must be enforced via repression, by silencing popular discontent and demands.

What then are the main, long-term social justice—or "human rights for the millions"—issues that urgently need to be addressed in China, if society is to be made more fundamentally stable and equitable in nature? Here is a brief list of four of the most pressing issues:

  • The country's medical care system needs to be completely redesigned to make it more accessible and available to ordinary citizens. For at least the past decade, after the hospital system was basically privatized and turned into a for-profit concern, the cost of medical treatment has been prohibitive for the majority of China's citizens, even in the cities. Under the present system, a major

illness can bankrupt an entire family within a few short weeks—and in many rural areas, there is no public healthcare system worth mentioning.
• The rural education system also needs to be completely overhauled, and for similar reasons. Both the quality and provision of education in the countryside is massively under-funded by the government, and school fees are often extremely high. The result is that poor rural families increasingly cannot afford to keep their children in school for the full nine-year period of compulsory education, and so child labor is on the rise in many parts of the country today. In addition, the under-educated migrant workforce is increasingly inadequate to the developing needs of the Chinese economy, and this problem will only get worse unless action is taken swiftly. After more than a decade of 10 percent-plus annual GDP growth, the government's failure to make a priority of providing decent medical care and rural education for its citizens is deplorable.
• The entrenched problem of official corruption, now endemic at every level of the administration, needs to be seriously and systematically addressed by the central government. Corruption by local officials is at the root of almost every major social injustice issue in the country today, and it is deeply resented by the great majority of ordinary citizens. The central government regularly attacks dissidents, civic action groups, and petitioners or whistleblowers and others as posing a "threat to social and political stability." In reality, the persistence of unchecked corruption at all levels of official life is what poses the primary threat to the country's stable and peaceful development, both now and in the future. Since one-party rule seems set to last for a long time, the only available counterweight to official corruption remains the emergence of a functioning civil society in China—something that is now happening despite government controls.
• The basic livelihood of hundreds of millions of urban and rural workers and their families needs to be guaranteed and protected, in terms of access to proper employment, enforcement of legal minimum pay and maximum working hours, and provision of safe working conditions. The appalling situation in China's coal mines, where several thousand miners continue to die needlessly each year as a direct result of mine bosses' callous disregard for workplace safety, and with the collusion of local officials who unlawfully invest in the mines, is only the most dramatic example. Similar conditions prevail throughout the country's vast construction industry and elsewhere, and the only effective remedy is for workers to be allowed to form effective self-protection organizations. Trade unions would be the most obvious form, but while legal prohibitions on such groups remain, workers should at least be allowed to form frontline work-safety committees, and also to engage in real collective bargaining with their employers aimed at negotiating minimally acceptable terms and conditions of employment.

Again looking ahead to the post-Olympics period: if the international community has less and less real influence and leverage nowadays over Beijing on how it treats its own citizens, does this mean that future prospects for human rights and greater social justice in China are bleak? Surprisingly enough, perhaps: far from it. For we are finally seeing, after three decades of economic reform, the emergence of new domestic social forces in China that may well have the will and the potential to transform the country's governance from the inside, and from the bottom up. For a variety of reasons, there is considerably more space for civic action of all kinds in society nowadays than even five or ten years ago. This is not the result of government steps toward liberalization: rather, it's because angry citizens are now demanding justice in much larger numbers, and more vocally, than ever before. Ordinary people across the country, in both town and countryside, are themselves creating this new and indispensable social space, through a wide range of collective rights campaigns and activities. All this is ultimately the outcome of three decades of highly inequitable economic reform in China, and where issues of social injustice are concerned, the chickens are now coming home to roost for the Chinese leadership.

NEW FORCES FOR CHANGE FROM WITHIN

In short, I believe that China is now entering a stage where progress toward greater social justice, including human and labor rights—or "human rights for the millions"—will henceforth be determined mainly as a result of internal forces and developments, with the international community playing a secondary (though still vital) role in events. In my view, this development is warmly to be welcomed, and I see two such new social forces, primarily, at work in China today.

First, there is now a recognizable workers' rights movement of considerable size taking shape in China, something that was scarcely conceivable only a decade ago. Tens of thousands of mass labor protests and other acts of worker unrest are taking place across the country each year, despite the continued strict legal prohibition on forming independent unions. These worker protests are mostly spontaneous in nature, and are neither coordinated nor interconnected, but they are having a real and tangible effect in promoting greater respect by employers, at local level, for the country's own labor laws. China's workers, and especially the 150 million or so migrant workforce (mostly female) from the countryside that provides the muscle for urban manufacturing and exports, are clearly on the move.

Workers are no longer playing the role of passive victim to China's economic success story, and instead are increasingly standing up for themselves and their rights. And the one-party state—which preys on the weak and isolated (the political dissidents, civil rights lawyers, Falun Gong and others) but fears the strong and numerous—is in turn showing the workers steadily increasing attention and respect as a social force. It is no coincidence that the start of 2008 saw the introduction of three new labor laws in China: the Labour Contract Law, the Law on Employment Promotion, and the Law on Labour Dispute Mediation and Arbitration. All of these new laws have, in various significant ways, raised the bar on employment standards and labor rights. (The main continuing problem is that employers and local authorities conspire to ignore such laws in practice; but here again, workers are challenging the system to live up to its own promises by bringing increasing numbers of labor rights lawsuit to court—and for the most part they are winning.) In the human rights movement, we have long known that, if properly applied, international pressure works; so it is heartening to report that in China today, pressure from domestic actors and forces is likewise starting to work.

Second, there is currently emerging in China a sizable, grassroots-based rights movement of great significance, one that is focused on issues of real and pressing concern to the local community and is therefore winning widespread popular support. Citizens around the country are forming pressure groups to campaign for the redress of local acts of injustice or bad governance, and they are increasingly taking their cases to the courts in the form of lawsuits against local government agencies and officials. Known in China as the *"weiquan"* movement—usually translated in English as the "rights defense movement"—it in many ways constitutes China's emerging civil rights movement. It shares many of the features of civil rights movements elsewhere—for example, the coalition of elite social groups, including civil rights lawyers, the news media and local legislators, alongside and in support of grassroots-based rights campaigners—a phenomenon that was also evident in the case of the Civil Rights Movement in the United States, despite the different issues involved.

Crucially, much of China's fast-growing *"weiquan"* movement is inspired by rising levels of popular indignation over the flagrant levels of official corruption seen across the country nowadays. Increasing income polarization may be an unavoidable feature of economic development, but official greed and contempt for rule of law is now directly ruining more and more Chinese citizens' basic livelihood—whether via unlawful land grabs, catastrophic pollution of the environment, or other widespread acts of malgovernance. More and more officials in China are nowadays acting as if they fear the party may be over tomorrow: grabbing as much as they can, without apparent concern for the probably irreversible decline in government legitimacy that their actions are prompting in the eyes of ordinary citizens.

What characterizes both these new social forces—the workers on the one hand, and the popular *"weiquan"* or civil rights movement on the other—is their shared commitment to peaceful and constitutional methods of social action and pressure for change. They have wisely, for the most part, avoided politicizing the very diverse social justice issues on which they campaign—even when, as is usually the case, these problems are the direct product of official corruption; and they have based their campaigns on the provisions of China's own laws. Both tactics are vital if these movements are to prosper and grow in the future, and they essentially boil down to demanding genuine rule of law in China. Again, these are popular, grassroots-based campaigns and concerns, and it is the first time in monitoring human rights in China for some 30 years that I have seen anything quite so positive and momentous occur.

TAKING THE LONGER VIEW

How can the international community best lend its support to these promising new developments taking place at the grassroots level across China? Here are a few pointers and suggestions:

- Western governments should give a high priority to pressing China, through the U.N. and the ILO, to ratify core international agreements and conventions on freedom of speech and association, notably the ICCPR and ILO Conventions No. 87 and 98. If Chinese citizens cannot freely associate to press for peaceful change and reform, the country will become more and more of a political powder keg on the world stage.
- Western governments should continue to press Beijing for the release of individual prisoners of conscience. The handing of such prisoner lists to senior Chinese officials should be restored as a routine component of all high-level diplomatic and governmental meetings with the Chinese leadership. As history has repeatedly shown, one freed individual can inspire millions of others.
- Western foundations should greatly increase the level of support they give to grassroots-based civic action groups of all kinds in China, whether environmental, civil rights, women's rights or labor-movement-related, while continuing to support a limited number of official projects via the more progressive government agencies. The overwhelming majority of these grassroots activist groups are both socially responsible and politically self-restrained, and their common goal is to develop a secure and stable rule of law in China. They are the country's main hope for the future.
- Multinationals operating in China, where independent trade unions are banned by law and labor is cheap and plentiful, have a moral duty to maintain strong codes of conduct and pursue effective corporate social responsibility programs. However, social justice in the workplace in China cannot be planned and executed from corporate boardrooms in Western capitals. The experience of all other countries where minimum labor standards have been won shows that there is no substitute for real trade unions, and that freedom of association is the indispensable key. China is no exception here, and there is no convenient short cut to real labor rights for hundreds of millions of people. China's workers are perfectly capable of protecting themselves, given the necessary rights and tools. What they need is support and encouragement to do so.
- In addition, both multinationals and consumers in the West need to recognize that, in order to really achieve better and more acceptable labor standards for ordinary working people in China, the cost of China's exported goods will inevitably have to rise. Increased productive efficiency can only go so far toward providing the funds needed to provide Chinese workers with acceptable pay, reasonable working hours, mandatory work-related insurance coverage and safe factory conditions. The real problem is that these goods are much too cheap—and under-priced Chinese goods in Western shopping malls means continued labor rights violations in China.
- Both citizens and governments in the West should recognize, moreover, that higher labor standards for Chinese workers will also directly benefit the workforces in their own countries. By making it possible for Chinese workers to enjoy minimum acceptable standards, Western citizens and consumers will find that their own jobs become more secure, the trend toward casualization and part-timing of labor will reduce, and working-class families in many countries will benefit as a result.

In conclusion, China's hosting of the Olympic Games may be momentous for reasons of national pride and as a symbol of the country's long-delayed emergence as a great power economically. But it is largely irrelevant to the real social and political issues facing China and its ordinary working population today. The foremost of these are, first, the continued sharp polarization of society in terms of basic livelihood and access to vital public services; and second, the steadily growing range of severe social injustice issues—mostly generated by official corruption—that affect huge numbers of citizens and are fuelling rising levels of popular discontent and anger.

Unless these urgent social problems are addressed by the central government, by imposing an effective system of public accountability on officials and by allowing civil society to develop as a real counterweight to the one-party system, China's Olympics slogan of "One World, One Dream" will probably end up being viewed by its people as merely one more cynical diversion from reality, to be added to the scrap-heap of similar political slogans used by the Party over the past sixty years and more.

Finally, Mr.Chairman, with your permission, I would like to draw the Commission's attention to an article drafted by my colleagues at China Labour Bulletin, Geoff Crothall and Han Dongfang. This article, which will be published in the forthcoming book, "China's Great Leap," provides a vivid analysis of the causes and conditions of the harsh environment in which Chinese migrant workers generally labor, both at the Olympic construction sites and across the country as a whole.

Thank you all for your time and attention.

———

PREPARED STATEMENT OF HON. SANDER LEVIN, A U.S. REPRESENTATIVE FROM MICHIGAN, CHAIRMAN, CONGRESSIONAL-EXECUTIVE COMMISSION ON CHINA

FEBRUARY 27, 2008

The Commission convenes this hearing to examine the likely impact of the 2008 Summer Olympics on human rights and the rule of law in China. In its Olympic bid documents and in its preparations for the 2008 Summer Games, China made commitments pertaining to human rights and the rule of law. Our witnesses today will help us to evaluate these commitments and to assess the openness with which China has allowed the rest of the world to monitor its progress in fulfilling them.

In the days before the International Olympic Committee voted to select Beijing as the site of the 2008 Olympics, there was consideration of human rights and related issues, as had been the case in previous deliberations about appropriate sites for the Olympics. China made a point of raising the link between human rights and the 2008 Games. On July 12, 2001, the state-run China Daily reported that Wang Wei, Secretary General of the Beijing Olympic bid committee, said, "We are confident that the Games coming to China not only promotes our economy, but also enhances all social conditions, including education, health and human rights." These words could not have been clearer. Human rights and the 2008 Olympics were linked before Beijing was awarded the Games, and China itself linked them.

Just yesterday, China's Foreign Minister announced that China is ready to resume the human rights dialogue with the United States that it broke off in 2004. This announcement underlines the relevance of this hearing, which was announced several weeks ago, and means that there is considerable and appropriate ground to cover today.

On press freedom, Beijing's bid documents stated, "(t)here will be no restrictions on journalists in reporting on the Olympic Games." At the same time, they also stated, "(t)here will be no restriction concerning the use of media material produced in China and intended principally for broadcast outside."

On openness in general, Beijing's Action Plan for the Olympics states, "in the preparation for the Games, we will be open in every aspect to the rest of the country and the whole world." On government transparency more specifically, Beijing's Action Plan for the Olympics states, "Government work will be open to public supervision and information concerning major Olympic construction projects shall be made public regularly."

This last point deserves extra attention because it underscores the importance of China's new Regulation on the Public Disclosure of Government Information, which takes effect on May 1 of this year. This new Regulation promises people in China the legal means to obtain access to government records related to construction, labor affairs, health and safety, the environment, and much more before the Games begin and also after. The Commission looks forward to reporting on the implementation of this important new Regulation in the weeks and months ahead.

Much of the world's attention also has focused on China's environment. Beijing's bid documents stated, "By 2008, the environmental quality in Beijing will be comparable to that of major cities in developed countries, with clean and fresh air, a beautiful environment, and healthy ecology. Meteorological observations in the area of Beijing in the past 10 years have indicated that July and August are good time to hold the Olympic Games."

I must note that China's security preparations for the Olympics also raise concerns. Congress banned the transfer of crime control equipment to China after the Tiananmen killings of 1989. Nonetheless, recent press reports describe the export from the United States to China of equipment identified as commercial, but with crime control applications. This merits attention because after the Olympics, high-technology surveillance products will be left in the hands of China's public security and state security organs, who may use them to monitor political activists, religious practitioners, and members of certain ethnic minority groups.

The Commission asked Under Secretary of Commerce for Industry and Security Mario Mancuso to testify today, but he is in India on official business and unfortunately could not join us. However he has offered to respond to questions in writing. A list is being prepared, and I invite members to add to it.

China does not want to be labeled as a gross violator of human rights. And yet it makes its determination to eliminate dissent painfully clear to the world. Thousands of prisoners of conscience languish in jail cells across China. Just in the last few weeks, China has detained individuals who have mentioned the Olympics when speaking out for human rights. Officials have cast their public-mindedness as a subversion of state power. These same authorities assert that raising concern over human rights in the context of the 2008 Games violates the Olympic spirit. Nothing could be farther from the truth. Fairness on the field of play, fair judgments and the opportunity to witness human potential unleashed to the fullest extent are the very essence of the Olympic spirit. They are also the essence of freedom and fundamental human rights.

In seeking the 2008 Olympics, China made specific commitments. Seven years have passed, and the Games begin in less than six months. This hearing is a necessary part of determining whether China is fulfilling its commitments. China is an increasingly important part of the international community, and it is vital that there be continuing assessment of its commitments, whether as a member of the WTO or as the awarded host of the Olympics. Other nations, including ours, have both the responsibility and a legitimate interest in ensuring compliance with those commitments.

PREPARED STATEMENT OF HON. BYRON DORGAN, A U.S. SENATOR FROM NORTH DAKOTA, CO-CHAIRMAN, CONGRESSIONAL-EXECUTIVE COMMISSION ON CHINA

FEBRUARY 27, 2008

Mr. Chairman, I want to commend you for holding this hearing today. It will explore what I believe has been a largely unexamined issue: whether the 2008 Olympics will in fact bring lasting benefits to the Chinese people by enhancing their human rights and accelerating rule of law reform.

The 2008 Olympics have focused the world's attention on China's support for repressive regimes, such as Sudan and Burma. And, this has been all for the good. Our government and the international community, however, have paid too little attention to the potential impact of the Games on the human rights of ordinary Chinese citizens.

China views the 2008 Olympics as not merely an international athletic event, but as recognition of its global economic, diplomatic and military power. It is a political event of great significance. It will confirm China's acceptance as a proud and prominent participant on the international stage. Whether Beijing will seize the opportunity presented by the Olympics to improve its record and recast its human rights legacy remains a vital open question.

Beijing lost its bid to host the 2000 Olympic Games, in part, because of the long shadow cast by the Chinese government's crackdown on the Tiananmen Square democracy movement in 1989.

Government negotiators worked to secure a better outcome for their second effort to the host the games. They were successful, in part, by promising the International Olympic Committee that China would commit itself to significant reforms. These included allowing international reporters unfettered access across the country, and substantial improvements in air quality. Today, however, foreign journalists say they and their Chinese colleagues and interviewees are being harassed. And, the smog in Beijing remains as thick as ever.

The Games are now just six months away. The human rights situation on the ground is deeply troubling. Already, China has begun detaining citizens who have tied the Olympics to their peaceful criticism of the government's human rights record. Recently, China jailed Hu Jia, a courageous dissident who did nothing more than address a hearing on the Olympics. The hearing was quite similar to this one, and before the European Parliament. China insists that Mr. Hu's actions violated its laws on state secrets. As a result, he was dragged from his home by state police agents and now sits in jail. His wife and three-month old daughter remain in their apartment under house arrest. Their telephone and Internet connections are cut.

Just last week, Yang Chunlin, an unemployed factory worker, went on trial for subversion in northeast China. Mr. Yang was arrested last year for reportedly helping nearby villagers seeking compensation for lost land. He had collected more than 10,000 signatures from local farmers. The signatures were for a letter which read, "We Want Human Rights, not the Olympics." Prosecutors have said that the letter stained China's international image, and that it amounted to subversion.

What if China had done the opposite? Instead of punishing Yang for his activism, what if the government had instead acknowledged his underlying message? Had that course been chosen, China would have improved its international image in one fell swoop. Instead, China further stained it.

Mr. Chairman, I would ask that the following list of political prisoners in China be entered into the hearing record. It is a short, representative list of individuals detained in recent years by the government for Olympics-related or other activities. The most important thing to notice about this list, Mr. Chairman, is that each of the people on it is in jail for having done nothing wrong. They did nothing wrong.

I am not only concerned by China's detention of citizen activists. I am also concerned about the treatment of large numbers of migrant workers who have been employed to manufacture Olympic merchandise and construct Olympic sites. These migrant workers, like millions of others across China, are required to work under the most hazardous conditions. They are routinely cheated out of their wages, and rarely have work-related medical insurance or labor contracts.

China has passed new and important legislation in the labor area, but implementation does not appear yet to be addressing the needs of those most in need of relief, those whom these laws were intended to protect. This Commission will remain focused on problems of implementation in the year to come.

The rights of workers, the right to speak freely, the right to challenge the government—all of these are enshrined in China's constitution. Yet, all of these are chronically violated. In such circumstances, it is crucial that we who can exercise these rights and defenses debate the reality in China, and question whether China is fulfilling its commitments on the Olympics.

PREPARED STATEMENT OF HON. DONALD A. MANZULLO, A U.S. REPRESENTATIVE FROM ILLINOIS, MEMBER, CONGRESSIONAL-EXECUTIVE COMMISSION ON CHINA

Mr. Chairman, thank you for calling this important hearing on the impact of the Beijing Olympics on human rights, the rule of law, and media freedom. I am delighted to be a part of the Congressional-Executive Commission and this first hearing. I believe that it is our duty as Members of Congress to do all we can to urge all nations to respect fundamental human rights and to protect life in all its forms. We must give voice to the voiceless and not shy from confronting oppression.

The People's Republic of China will for the first time in its history host the Olympic Games, which is one of the most prestigious events in the world. Undoubtedly for the Chinese, the Games symbolize much more than athletic prowess; it is after all a golden opportunity for China to demonstrate to the world its emergence as a global power. And for the rest of the world, the Games represent an important occasion to urge China to continue making progress in its reforms.

Unfortunately, some of China's actions both domestically and on the international arena have led me to believe that they are counterproductive to its stated goal of becoming a more responsible player in the international community. On a range of issues ranging from human rights abuses and Internet censorship to arms sales in Darfur and forced abortion, China has proved to be less than the responsible stakeholder it claims to be. Even on the environment, China's rapid development has left an unmistakable imprint of pollution and harm. Part of the problem for China is its immense size and influence; everything it does has a global impact.

Mr. Chairman, I welcome this Commission's inquiry into China's human rights record and respect for the rule of law. I originally supported permanent normalized trade relations for China because I believed it would help speed reforms and liberalization. Eight years after the passage of PNTR, China's progress on human rights, religious prosecution, forced abortion, and censorship remains mixed. I am disappointed by this lack of progress; however, I still believe proactive engagement is the best path to take to encourage more progress.

Thank you for holding this hearing. I look forward to the testimonies.

PREPARED STATEMENT OF HON. CHRISTOPHER H. SMITH, A U.S. REPRESENTATIVE FROM NEW JERSEY, MEMBER, CONGRESSIONAL-EXECUTIVE COMMISSION ON CHINA

FEBRUARY 27, 2008

Thank you, Mr. Chairman, and good afternoon to everyone.

Mr. Chairman, thank you for calling this hearing. I remember that you were one of the Congressmen who in 2000 led the fight to create this Commission, ensuring that Congress not lose its focus on human rights in China. The fact that the Olympics will be held in China this summer should be of grave concern to Congress.

A few weeks ago, the New York Times reported the arrest of a 34-year-old Chinese dissident named Hu Jia.

Mr. Hu's crime? Using his home computer to disseminate information on human rights violations. He joins a huge, ever-growing number of cyber dissidents who today, in China, are being hauled off to jail simply for promoting democracy and human rights.

The Times article suggests the obvious: in the run-up to the Beijing Olympics in August, the PRC is using its iron fists to eradicate dissent.

Even Mr. Hu's wife and 2-month old daughter are now under house arrest, prompting the Times to note that their baby is "probably the youngest political prisoner in China."

How sad is that?

But in this particular case we can take direct action against this abuse. I am afraid that many American companies, like Google, Microsoft, and Yahoo!, have cooperated with the Chinese government in turning the Internet into a tool of surveillance and censorship. Last year I introduced the Global Online Freedom Act to prevent U.S. high-tech Internet companies from turning over to the Chinese police information that identifies individual Internet users, and to require them to disclose how the Chinese version of their search engines censors the Internet. In October, the Foreign Affairs Committee approved the bill, and we are hoping to move it to the floor of the House soon.

The fact of the matter is that the scale of human rights violations perpetrated by the Chinese government exceeds that of any other government on earth.

In China, forced abortion is pervasive as a means of enforcing the government's draconian one child per couple policy, a policy which has made brothers and sisters illegal. Government officials have coerced compliance with this inhuman policy through a system marked by pervasive propaganda, mandatory monitoring of women's reproductive cycles, mandatory contraception, mandatory birth permits, coercive fines for failure to comply, and, in many cases, forced sterilization and forced abortion. The Chinese government's population planning laws and regulations contravene international human rights standards at every level, not only through the horror of forced abortion, but also by limiting the number of children that women may bear, by coercing compliance with population targets through heavy fines, and by discriminating against "out-of-plan" children.

The one-child policy has led to a social plague of gendercide, the annihilation of tens of millions of girls, just because they were girls. According to the Chinese government's official figures, the ratio of boys to girls born in China is 120 to 100. In some provinces of China it is 140 to 100, and even higher. And these are official figures; the real figures are probably higher.

The Chinese government has no notion of religious freedom. It arrests members of the house church movement merely for gathering in each other's homes to read Scripture and pray. This happens all the time. Seven days ago, the China Aid Association reported the arrest of more than 40 house church members in Inner Mongolia. Eleven days ago, China Aid reported that 21 major house church leaders were sent to labor camps in Shandong.

The Chinese government even invents human rights violations that no one else had thought of. Two weeks ago, ABC News' "20/ 20" reported that dissected bodies, coated in plastic, which are being displayed in touring shows across America, were the bodies of executed prisoners, sold, by the very officials who had a hand in killing them, on a black market for dead bodies. Here too the crime touches American soil, so I have requested a hearing on this matter, written to the Attorney General requesting an investigation, and am drafting legislation to require independent experts to verify the identity, manner of death, and consent to display, of any corpses to be commercially displayed in the United States.

In China there is no freedom of speech, press, or assembly, and internationally recognized labor rights simply don't exist.

Despite enormous concessions by the West, robust trade with the United States, Europe, Africa and Latin America, and WTO accession, the Chinese government's brutal crackdown on religious, labor, environmental, and democracy activists has continued, unabated, and even worsened, since the Tiananmen Square Massacre almost 20 years ago!

Men and women of conscience—so many of China's best and bravest, who if freed could transform their country—are today in Laogai—the Chinese Gulag.

Given the nature and scale of human rights violations by the Chinese government, it is a shame that the Olympics will be held in China. But I believe we cannot let the Olympics pass without asserting our solidarity with the victims—those who have been hurt, or even destroyed, by the myriad human rights violations perpetrated by the Chinese government.

Their sufferings must not be forgotten!

I look forward to learning from the representatives of so many distinguished human rights NGOs what is the best way we can speak up on behalf of the imprisoned in the run-up to the Olympics.

The Olympics will certainly not be a time to remain silent. I remember how Wei Jingsheng, the great Chinese democracy activist who spent more than 14 years in prison, told me in Beijing about a paradox. When Americans or others boldly and tenaciously demand that the Chinese government release prisoners, some do get out, others get more lenient treatment. On the other hand, he said, when you forget us, kow-tow to the government, or engage in diplomatic niceties, the guards aren't nice to us in return, they beat us more.

The human rights dissidents of China need friends and advocates. They need us to turn this window of pre-Olympic opportunity into a season of hope, justice, and freedom. No one has more clout than the representatives of the human rights NGOs present today. Together we need to find our voice—for them.

PREPARED STATEMENT OF HON. CHUCK HAGEL, A U.S. SENATOR FROM NEBRASKA, MEMBER, CONGRESSIONAL-EXECUTIVE COMMISSION ON CHINA

FEBRUARY 27, 2008

The Congressional-Executive Commission on China (CECC) meets today to discuss the 2008 Summer Olympic Games and its impact on human rights and the rule of law in China. This is the first Commission hearing under its new leadership, and I thank my distinguished colleagues, Chairman Sander Levin and Co-Chairman Byron Dorgan, for bringing us together here today. I look forward to working with you, as well as my fellow Ranking Member, Congressman Chris Smith, and each of the Commission members to continue the good work and prominent reputation that the Commission has established over the past seven years.

I would like to thank each of the distinguished witnesses for coming today to discuss these important issues, and I look forward to hearing your testimony.

There is no strategic relationship more important to the United States than China. U.S.-China relations cover the full arc of our national interests — economic growth, national security, financial, social, and regional stability, as well as political reform, individual rights, the rule of law and religious freedom. From civil and intellectual property rights to the balance of trade, we continue to have clear differences with the Chinese government.

In the recently published 2007 CECC Annual Report, the Commission found that China's record of compliance with international human rights standards has been mixed. The Commission does recognize the progress that China has made in bringing its legal statutes and regulations nominally in line with international standards. These reforms may one day provide the legal backdrop for constraining the arbitrary exercise of government authority in China.

China should also be commended for its achievements in the economic realm. Its success in lifting more than 400 million Chinese citizens out of extreme poverty since the early 1980's should not be overlooked. However, China's progress on civil and political rights has unfortunately not kept pace with its economic progress. Significant human rights abuses and problems with the application of the rule of law in China need to be addressed.

In the 2007 CECC Annual Report, the Commission found that despite legal and regulatory reform, the changes "have not necessarily translated into the everyday practice of local law enforcement." Major concerns remain over religious freedom, property rights, corruption, and the right of political dissent. China will not be a full and responsible member of the global community, nor will it reach its own potential, until political reforms move forward as economic development has done.

The 2008 Summer Olympics present China and the international community with a significant opportunity for progress and dialogue—especially with regard to human rights and the rule of law in China. Beijing has made a number of important commitments to domestic political and legal reforms in the lead-up to the Olympics—among them, promises to advance religious, economic, civil, and social freedoms inside China. As a responsible member of the international community, China should meet those important commitments.

The international community should also take advantage of this opportunity to enter into expanded dialogue with China on areas of both disagreement and of mutual concern. The Olympics present a chance to take another step toward engagement and common purpose, but we need to remember that it is but one step on this path.

Lasting and stable progress on liberalization and domestic reform takes time. Change does not happen overnight, and our disagreements with China will not be resolved by the time the Olympics leave Beijing. At some point, late this summer, the Olympics will be over, but our differences over human rights, the rule of law, trade issues, and others will likely still remain.

The global community should use this opportunity to help frame a constructive, long-term, strategic relationship with China where our differences can be aired and areas of mutual concern can be found. In the coming months, we must be realistic, balanced, measured, focused and clear headed in our approach to China.

The Commission looks forward to hearing the testimony from this distinguished panel of witnesses. Thank you all for coming. We appreciate your time and presentations.

———

PREPARED STATEMENT OF HON. GORDON H. SMITH, A U.S. SENATOR FROM OREGON, MEMBER, CONGRESSIONAL-EXECUTIVE COMMISSION ON CHINA

FEBRUARY 27, 2008

I wish to thank Chairman Levin for holding this important hearing. I also wish to thank our distinguished guests who will testify before the Commission today. I appreciate their willingness to join the Commission today and answer questions as they may arise.

2008 is a crucial year for China as it hosts the Summer Olympics. The moment has finally come for Beijing to demonstrate to the world that it is a respectful and responsible member of the global community. China is quickly finding itself a dominant regional power with considerable influence around the world. But to become a world leader, Beijing must demonstrate its ability to lead in a responsible manner.

2008 is China's year of opportunity to prove that it can handle the benefits and responsibilities newly bestowed upon it. Benefits include a booming economy and reformed financial and industrial sectors. Responsibilities include the necessity of respecting human rights, adhering strongly to the rule of law, and abiding by the norms of the international community. It is vital that Beijing end its political and economic support of rogue regimes around the world, from North Korea to Burma to Sudan. Unfortunately, China's behavior is troubling; opposition to strong UN action on Iran or Darfur, the mass relocation of people, suppression of dissidents, and the censorship of Chinese journalists are just a few of several recent troubling events.

Beijing must also take greater measures to respect the minority religions in the country. Religious persecution must end before China will ever be recognized as an honorable world power. The Chinese people should feel comfortable practicing their own religion in a fashion of their own choosing. I urge the Chinese government to allow all religious sects to worship freely and without fear of persecution.

The 2008 Summer Olympics will be an excellent opportunity for Beijing to demonstrate that China can be a responsible power with an open society, not only for the countless visitors, but for the Chinese people. I look forward to hearing our expert's projection on how the Olympics will impact China's society. While I would like to remain optimistic, I am not convinced the Games will have the positive impact many are hoping for.

SUBMISSIONS FOR THE RECORD

PREPARED STATEMENT AND RESPONSES TO COMMISSION'S QUESTIONS BY MARIO
MANCUSO, UNDER SECRETARY FOR INDUSTRY AND SECURITY, U.S. DEPARTMENT OF
COMMERCE

MAY 1, 2008

I. BACKGROUND ON U.S. CRIME CONTROL POLICY

U.S. crime control policy fits within the broader U.S. foreign policy objectives of
promoting human rights abroad. The Bureau of Industry and Security (BIS) at the
U.S. Department of Commerce is entrusted with the responsibility of licensing the
export of crime control and detection items to most countries around the world, pursuant to the Export Administration Act (EAA) of 1979 as amended.

Pursuant to Section 6(n) of the EAA, the U.S. Government requires a license for
the export of crime control and detection instruments, equipment, related technology, and software on the Commerce Control List (CCL) to all destinations, except
Australia, Japan, New Zealand, and members of the North Atlantic Treaty Organization (NATO). Certain restraint-type devices, such as handcuffs, and discharge-
type items, such as tasers, however, require a license to all countries except Canada.
The list of items controlled for crime control reasons, and countries subject to these
controls, is compiled with the concurrence of the Department of State.

In addition to these licensing requirements, it is important to note the policy BIS
applies to all applications for licenses to export items controlled for crime control
reasons. BIS implements a policy of denial for any license application to export spe-
cially designed implements of torture, thumbscrews, and thumbcuffs. Furthermore,
BIS applies a general policy of denial for license applications to export crime control
items to countries in which the government engages in the consistent pattern of
gross violations of internationally recognized human rights. For other countries, BIS
considers license applications for crime control items favorably, unless there is civil
disorder in the country or region, or there is evidence that the government may
have violated internationally recognized human rights. In making all of the above
determinations, BIS determines whether the judicious use of export controls would
be helpful in deterring the development of a consistent pattern of such violations,
distancing the U.S. Government from such abuses, and avoiding the contribution to
civil disorder in a country or region. BIS crime control policy can be found in the
Export Administration Regulations (EAR) in 15 C.F.R.§§ 742.7 and 742.11.

II. CRIME CONTROL POLICY: CHINA

As the U.S. Government has certain positive exceptions to its crime control licensing policy for some of its closest allies, there are also certain countries, such as
China, Indonesia, Rwanda, and the Ivory Coast, for which U.S. policy is more stringent. With respect to China, Congress passed the Foreign Relations Authorization
Act for Fiscal Years 1990-1991, Title IX of which is often referred to as the
"Tiananmen Sanctions". Pursuant to the Tiananmen Sanctions, the issuance of licenses for the export of any crime control or detection instruments or equipment
controlled on the CCL for crime control reasons has been suspended to China. Only
the President may terminate this suspension by reporting to Congress that China
has conducted political reforms or that it is in the national interest to terminate
such a suspension. The President has not exercised this authority to date.

Detailed below are specific responses to the Congressional-Executive Commission
on China's inquiries that seek to explain the place of China in BIS's overall crime
control policy.

III. RESPONSES TO QUESTIONS

Question 1: The current list of crime control items that are indefinitely suspended
from export to China includes items such as handcuffs and fingerprinting equipment. Please briefly describe how the Bureau of Industry and Security (BIS)
ensure[s] this list is current and takes into account changing technologies relating
to crime control equipment, which have occurred since the "Tiananmen Square"
crime control restrictions went into effect 18 years ago. How many reviews of this
list have you conducted over the last 18 years, what prompted those reviews, and
what were the results of such reviews (i.e. in terms of whether items were added
or removed from the list)?

Response: BIS conducts an annual review of EAR crime controls, and all foreign policy-based export controls, in the context of the Foreign Policy Report to Congress. Under the provision of Section 6 of the EAA as amended, export controls maintained for foreign policy purposes require annual extension. Each year BIS publishes a notice in the Federal Register requesting public comments on the effects of foreign policy-based export controls. The notice states that BIS is reviewing those controls to determine whether they should be modified, rescinded, or extended. To help make these determinations, BIS seeks public comments on how existing foreign policy-based export controls have affected exporters and the general public. Over the years, BIS has received few comments on the controls on crime control items. The last such comment was received in October 2004 and was a statement of support for our high level of crime controls and an exhortation to win more multilateral support for human rights controls.

In addition, as part of a larger review of the entire Commerce Control List (CCL), BIS has proactively initiated a comprehensive review of our crime control regulations. The Department has published a Notice of Inquiry in the Federal Register (73 FR 14769 of March 19, 2008) specifically seeking public comments by June 17, 2008 on the crime control export and reexport license requirements contained in the EAR. In particular, BIS is seeking public input on whether the scope of items currently subject to crime control license requirements should be revised to add or remove items. The Notice specifically seeks comment on whether items such as biometric devices, integrated security systems, and training software, specifically firearms training software, should be subject to crime control licensing requirements. BIS is also seeking public comments on whether the destinations to which crime control license requirements apply should be revised.

Potential changes to crime controls would not be limited to China. Control of the export of items for crime control reasons predates, and is not limited to, China, but applies to a wide range of countries, such as North Korea and Burma. The Tiananmen Sanctions require Commerce to prohibit, absent Presidential waiver, export of any items classified as crime control items to China. In other words, the Tiananmen Sanctions were based on the already existing crime control regulations that required licenses for the export of crime control items to many countries, including China, by prohibiting such items from being exported.

Some of the past changes to the CCL include: (i) removing thumbcuffs from Export Control Classification Number (ECCN) 0A982 and placing them into ECCN 0A983 (2007); (ii) adding pepper spray to ECCN 1A984 as a result of a commodity jurisdiction decision by the Department of State 2004; (iii) expanding controls on restraint devices and on discharge type arms controlled under ECCNs 0A982 and 0A985, and creating ECCN 0A978 for Saps and ECCNµ0A979 for shields and helmets (2000); and (iv) interpreting Tasers to be controlled as a discharge type arm under ECCN 0A985 (1994).

Question 2: Export administration regulations provide that the "judicious use of export controls is intended to deter the development of a consistent pattern of human rights abuses, distance the United States from such abuses and avoid contributing to civil disorder in a country or region." Please briefly explain how BIS monitors developments in China to ensure that U.S. companies are not contributing to "the development of a consistent pattern of human rights abuses" through the export of their products. Does BIS attempt to conduct its own fact-finding to determine whether the sale of a certain product to China has or will likely have an adverse impact on human rights in China? If so, please describe briefly how BIS conducts this fact-finding. If not, on whose fact-finding does BIS depend? If externally sourced findings were deficient, would BIS have any way to know?

Response: Under authority delegated by the President, the Secretary of State designates nations guilty of particularly severe violations of religious freedom as countries of particular concern under the International Religious Freedom Act of 1998 (H.R. 2431) and its amendment of 1999 (Public Law 106-55). In addition, in compliance with Sections 116(d) and 502B(b) of the Foreign Assistance Act of 1961 as amended, and Section 504 of the Trade Act of 1974, the Department of State submits Country Reports on Human Rights Practices annually to the Congress. The designations and findings of the Department of State with respect to human rights concerns provide the foreign policy guidance to BIS with respect to China. In addition, under the EAA, the Department of State has joint jurisdiction and responsibility for the CCL and the licenses that BIS issues for items controlled for crime control reasons on the CCL. The Department of State's participation in the review of all applications for individual licenses from BIS, including those for crime control reasons, provides the foreign policy guidance to BIS with respect to whether the sale of a certain product to China has or will likely have an adverse impact on human rights in China. As part of the review process, the Department of State considers the human rights record for the export destination.

Question 3: Please briefly describe what factors other than impact on human rights BIS considers when determining whether a specific crime control item should be restricted from export to China. Specifically, how much weight is given to those other factors relative to the weight given to human rights concerns, and how is that weight assigned?

Response: Pursuant to the Tiananmen Sanctions, the Department of Commerce implements a policy of denial of export license applications for items that are controlled on the CCL for crime control reasons. There is only one very limited circumstance in which specific crime control items may be temporarily exported to China. BIS does authorize the temporary export of defective Chinese-origin commercial rifle scopes from the United States to China for repair and return to the United States. Such warranty items are not operational at the time of their return for repair to China. As these items were manufactured in China, their return for repair and export back to the U.S. customer has no impact on the human rights situation in China.

Question 4: It appears that some items, such as surveillance equipment and routers, have not been included on the list because they are not designed solely to serve a "law enforcement purpose" and may be used for legitimate civilian purposes. Please explain the rationale for why such items are not currently on the list. Some products may be used primarily for "law enforcement purposes," even though their original design may not be solely for that purpose. How does BIS account for this? How much weight is given to evidence, if any, that either the seller knows such item will be used for "law enforcement purposes" or has marketed it for such purpose?

Response: Items primarily associated with human rights abuses, such as instruments of torture, are controlled for crime control reasons. In addition, items designed exclusively or primarily for law enforcement purposes are generally also controlled for crime control reasons because they could be used to abuse internationally recognized human rights. The intent of crime control regulations is to support U.S. foreign policy to promote the observance of human rights throughout the world. These controls are generally not limited, or specifically geared, to law enforcement or police activities. Not all items used by law enforcement are susceptible to human rights abuses. Conversely, in practice, license applications for many crime control items, such as scopes and shotguns, are not destined for police or government agencies but instead for sporting use. Items that are not currently controlled for crime control reasons are not on the list because, so far as BIS is aware, they do not meet the aforementioned criteria.

Routers and surveillance equipment have significant use in commercial environments. This is especially so for routers. With respect to surveillance systems, these can be as simple as the cameras and monitors used in banks, stores, and sporting arenas, or they can be larger integrated systems such as those used at ports or factory sites. Moreover, a review of the Internet shows that a number of countries, including China, manufactures and openly markets many of these systems and their components. However, technologies and markets for items change and in BIS's March 19 Federal Register Notice of Inquiry, one of the items about which we specifically request comments is integrated security systems.

BIS has initiated the current comprehensive evaluation of the crime control regulations to examine what new technologies are currently available in the marketplace, and what additions or deletions might be proposed in order to enhance the current controls.

Question 5: High-tech companies around the world are helping the Chinese government design and install one of the most comprehensive public surveillance systems ever for the 2008 Olympic Summer Games in Beijing. The Commerce Department reportedly has said that American companies' involvement in such projects does not run afoul of the post Tiananmen ban on providing China with "crime control or detection instruments or equipment." At the same time, the Commerce Department has recently conducted a review of its policies on the sale of crime-control gear to China. Please explain briefly what triggered the review. If helping the Chinese government design and install these public surveillance systems does not cause an American company to run afoul of the ban, then there must have been something else that triggered the review.

Response: The current crime control Notice of Inquiry was not a result of an increase in interest in the Chinese market or any actions of the Chinese government, but instead a determination that a much more detailed review of all aspects of crime control items, including the destinations to which the controls apply, license exceptions, and new technologies, was due. BIS is also undertaking a larger review of the CCL to ensure our controls are keeping pace with technological innovation and changing international economic conditions. Review of crime controls is included in this effort as well.

BIS has seen an increase in interest in the Chinese security-related market, with some of it certainly connected to the Olympics. However, China is a large, multi-faceted market and items of interest include explosive detection systems for airports, X-ray systems for packages and bags for people entering buildings or arenas, biometric-controlled entrance and lock systems, fire protection, rescue equipment, and radiation detection systems. Many of these items are not subject to export controls but are related to public safety. Those that are subject to export controls and controlled for reasons other than crime control can be approved for legitimate end-uses in China. For example, Commerce, with interagency review, has approved export licenses for explosive detection systems to Beijing International Airport and other airports in China.

Question 6: If BIS' review was prompted by a prospective determination of increased "human rights risk" and increased likelihood of companies' running afoul of the ban due to changes in the environment in which firms operate (rather than change in company behavior or activities), please identify the human rights risk assessment method, index or indicators the department relies upon. Please also explain the method the department uses to relate levels of risk to corresponding courses of action with respect to export controls.

Response: As noted in response to question #4, BIS has initiated the current comprehensive evaluation of the crime control regulations to examine what new technologies are currently available in the marketplace, and what additions or deletions might be proposed in order to enhance the current controls. The goal of the review is to ensure that the Commerce crime control regulations are up to date and that Commerce is knowledgeable about the most current technologies that may have a crime control application.

Question 7: The surveillance equipment sold by Western companies that will remain in China after the Olympics will leave Chinese authorities with tools that are newer and better than ever before to track dissidents, and not just criminals. Please describe, in your judgment, how significant a role export controls can play in mitigating that risk.

Response: To the extent that items are controlled on the CCL for crime control reasons, they are subject to a licensing policy of denial if destined to China. If the on-going review of Commerce crime controls leads to the identification of certain surveillance-related equipment, processing equipment, software, or system upgrades that need to be controlled for crime control reasons, then potential upgrades or software, even for previously exported systems, would require licensing and would be subject to denial policy under the Tiananmen Sanctions. Such controls would only impact U.S. and foreign companies exporting or reexporting crime control items subject to the EAR.

For items that are controlled on the CCL for national security or other reasons, reviewing agencies evaluate the end-user and make a determination in the course of adjudicating the license application. For example, if an item requires a license for reasons other than crime control, such as a thermal imaging camera that is controlled for national security reasons, and the end-use is one that poses human rights concerns, that would be a factor to be considered along with national security and non-proliferation concerns when reviewing the license application. Some controlled items, such as X-ray screeners and bomb detection equipment for airports, have legitimate security and public safety uses, that do not raise human rights concerns, that the U.S. Government, in particular the Federal Aviation Administration, promotes.

Question 8: The autumn issue of the magazine of China's public security ministry listed places of religious worship and Internet cafes as locations to install new surveillance cameras. When BIS learns of information such as this, what standard procedures are triggered? What alternatives have been identified for responding to it?

Response: When such information comes to the attention of the Executive Branch, the Department of State factors it into their overall human rights policy and evaluation of export license applications. Based on BIS's technical review to date, it appears much of this equipment is made in China, and the components of surveillance systems are widely available. The current BIS crime control review, however, does single out complete surveillance systems as a new technology possibly warranting control for crime control reasons. The crime control Notice of Inquiry specifically addresses such systems. Please see also the answer to question #2.

Question 9: On December 28, 2007, the International Herald Tribune quoted a "Commerce Department official who insisted on anonymity" as saying that "the sale of crime control gear to China is on a special, fast-track review." Please comment.

Response: The statement in the article is not accurate with regard to our crime control policy for China. As discussed in the response to question #3, BIS denies export license applications for items that are controlled on the CCL for crime control reasons. Under this licensing policy of denial, no other factors are considered. BIS is seeking comments on a review of the crime control list.

Question 10: The International Herald Tribune Reported on December 28, 2007 that BIS "bars exports whose sole use is law enforcement, like equipment for detecting fingerprints at crime scenes. But video systems are allowed if they are "industrial or civilian intrusion alarm, traffic or industrial movement control or counting systems,' according to the regulations." Do all systems so allowed comply fully with the spirit of the post Tiananmen export control laws?

Response: Yes. As discussed in the response to question #3, BIS denies export license applications for items that are controlled on the CCL for crime control reasons. Moreover, BIS has denied licenses for items controlled for other reasons to public security apparatus in China.

The article misinterprets the exception in the EAR "for industrial or civilian intrusion alarm, traffic or industrial movement and control or counting systems." This exception applies only to certain imaging cameras that contain certain controlled "focal plane arrays," which exempts the cameras from control under ECCN 6A003. This exception is not in any way tied to the Tiananmen Sanctions but instead is a note agreed upon by members of the Wassenaar Arrangement. As video systems are currently not controlled for crime control reasons, they are not subject to the Tiananmen Sanctions, which did not require imposing a licensing requirement on all commodities destined for the police. China makes many video systems and related components. As noted in earlier responses, our Notice of Inquiry seeks comments on whether the current list of items is adequate given changing technologies.

Question 11: China last winter created a nationwide "safe cities" program, establishing surveillance camera networks in more than 600 cities across China. Does this program figure into BIS' review and possible revision of export controls? If so, how?

Response: The BIS crime control review is not specifically directed toward China. As discussed in response to question #2, the designations and findings of the Department of State with respect to human rights concerns provide the foreign policy guidance to BIS with respect to China. In addition, the Department of State has joint jurisdiction and responsibility for the CCL and the licenses that BIS issues for items controlled for crime control reasons on the CCL.

Specifically regarding urban video surveillance systems, such systems are not unique to China or even to law enforcement activities. The public comments on the Notice of Inquiry on crime control items will help inform the United States Government's view on controls on such systems.

Question 12: Media outlets have reported that China lacks enough security guards to watch the video feeds from so many cameras. As a result, security industry executives report that Chinese authorities have been shopping for foreign computer systems that automatically analyze the information. How has BIS responded or intend to respond to this development?

Response: The current BIS crime control review does single out complete surveillance systems as a new technology possibly warranting control for crime control reasons. The Notice of Inquiry specifically addresses such systems and public comments will help inform the United States Government's view.

Question 13: Part of the sales pitches from American security companies is that their systems can protect the local police against false allegations of police abuse. Does this figure into BIS' review of export controls? If so, how? If not, why not?

Response: The current BIS crime control review does single out complete surveillance systems as a new technology possibly warranting control for crime control reasons. The Notice of Inquiry specifically addresses such systems and public comments will help inform the United States Government's view.

Question 14: On August 8, 2007, the Department of Commerce co-sponsored a webinar entitled "Understanding and Accessing the Security Market in China" (http://*www.buyusa.gov/eme/chinawebinar.html*) described as "providing U.S. electronic and physical security manufacturers valuable insight into this dynamic market, including entry-strategies and long-term market penetration plans" (http://*www.siaonline.org/research/index.cfm# Webinar*). Please describe the consultation with BIS that went into this program, and the extent to which BIS' input was reflected in the hour-long final product, available on line (http://*www.siaonline.orp/international/china security webinar.wmv*). Do programs such as this act at cross-purposes with BIS' current review and mandate?

Response: As part of the Commerce webinar, International Trade Administration presentations included: "Market Entry Strategies" and "Intellectual Property Rights in China," which appear to be aimed at the public safety-related market writ large and not any particular technology or sector such as the video market. In addition, BIS's export control attaché in Beijing gave a presentation on the "Tiananmen Sanctions and the Export of Crime Control Items to China." As the overall public security and safety market is a varied one, these presentations provided both the market opportunities and export control requirements associated with exporting certain technologies to China, which is consistent with the mandate of BIS.

CASES OF POLITICAL IMPRISONMENT IN CHINA

LIST OF POLITICAL PRISONERS SUBMITTED BY SENATOR BYRON DORGAN

1. **Hu Jia:** A prominent activist who has advocated on behalf of HIV/AIDS patients, environmental issues, and other rights defenders, Hu was detained by Chinese authorities on December 27, 2007, on suspicion of "inciting subversion of state power." Hu's detention may be linked to comments he made at a European Parliament hearing that were critical of China's hosting of the Olympics.

2. **Yang Chunlin:** As a land rights activist, Yang reportedly collected more than 10,000 signatures from farmers for a letter titled "We Want Human Rights, Not the Olympics," protesting the farmers' loss of land. Yang was detained in July 2007, and stood trial on charges of "inciting subversion of state power," on February 19.

3. **Wu Lihong:** An environmental activist from Jiangsu province, Wu spent more than a decade documenting pollution in Lake Tai, including providing environmental information to the government and the media. Shortly after Wu was detained in April 2007, Lake Tai experienced one of the worst blue-algae blooms, with millions of area residents without water for a few days. Wu was sentenced in August 2007 to three years in prison on the pretext of extortion and fraud.

4. **Guo Feixiong:** Guo is a prominent lawyer who was active in helping ordinary Chinese citizens defend their rights. In November 2007, Guo was sentenced to five years in prison for "illegal operation of a business," for allegedly distributing a publication without the necessary government license. The publication, which concerned a political scandal, reportedly angered local officials.

5. **Ronggyal Adrag:** A Tibetan nomad, Adrag was detained in August 2007 after he walked onto the speakers' stage at a horse-racing festival and called for the Dalai Lama's return to Tibet, the release of the Panchen Lama identified by the Dalai Lama, and Tibetan independence. In October, a court sentenced him to eight years in prison on the charge of "inciting splittism."

6. **Adrug Lupoe:** A nephew of Ronggyal Adrag, Adrug Lupoe is a monk who was sentenced by the same court to 10 years' imprisonment on charges of splittism and espionage. He allegedly helped two other men attempt to send digital photos out of China of the local security crackdown.

7. **Nurmemet Yasin:** He is an ethnic Uighur writer from Xinjiang who wrote a short story in 2004 about a caged bird who chooses suicide over living without freedom. Chinese authorities viewed the story as an attack on government policy in Xinjiang, and sentenced him in 2005 to 10 years in prison for "inciting splittism."

ATTACHMENT: AN APPEAL FROM THE TIANANMEN MOTHERS TO THE GOVERNMENT: SET A TIMETABLE FOR DIALOGUE ON THE JUNE FOURTH MASSACRE

[SUBMITTED BY SHARON HOM]

On the eve of the Eleventh National People's Congress and the Chinese People's Political Consultative Conference, we, a group of mothers of those killed in the June Fourth Massacre and, therefore, victims ourselves, earnestly request the following of you, the newly elected representatives of the NPC and the CPPCC:

On behalf of those who lost their lives during the June Fourth Massacre, we seek justice and equity to soothe the wounds of history. We wholeheartedly implore each of you: do not disregard the great trust that has been placed in you, do not insult your mission as representatives. Instead, we urge you, the two Congresses, to carry out a direct, equal, and sincere dialogue on the issue of the June Fourth Massacre with the victims and victims' families.

This is the eleventh time we have made an appeal to the NPC and CPPCC sessions. You who serve as the people's representatives and hold sacred legislative power: if you have any trace of conscience left, if your hearts retain even the smallest amount of sympathy, then how can you be so callous and indifferent?

In the past years, to facilitate this dialogue, we repeatedly requested the impartial and rational resolution of the following three points:

1. That the Standing Committee of the NPC form a specialized investigation committee on the June Fourth Massacre. Such committee should conduct an independent, open, and impartial investigation into the June Fourth Massacre and openly publish the results of the investigation, including the names and numbers of those killed in the June Fourth Massacre.

2. That the Standing Committee of the NPC require the bureau in charge of the June Fourth Massacre to issue a public apology to the family of each casualty of the Massacre in accordance with the law. The Standing Committee of the NPC should draft and pass a specialized "Law on the Compensation of Victims of the June Fourth Massacre" and give the victims and relatives of the June Fourth Massacre their lawful compensation.

3. The Standing Committee of the NPC should designate a prosecutorial organ to file and investigate cases from the June Fourth Massacre, and punish those found responsible in accordance with the law.

At the same time, we have repeatedly stated: "Issues remaining after June Fourth must be resolved through the legal system, in accordance with the law, without interference by any party, faction or individual. They must not be resolved according to the pattern of previous political campaigns, after which the government has always issued its own account of a 're-evaluation and exoneration.' In light of this, we call upon the National People's Congress to make use of the legislative process to discuss, review and issue a resolution on June Fourth issues."

However, we are disappointed that our requests, year after year, have come to nothing. Now that the 19th anniversary of June Fourth is approaching, and the splendid Olympic Games will be held in Beijing, China's capital, people will say: "This is a government that has sent tanks and armored vehicles into its capital to kill countless innocent students and civilians; a government that for more than 18 long years has not dared to confront the aftermath of the tragedy and has repeatedly refused dialogue with the victims' family members. How can this government face the whole world? Is it really possible that, as the host of the 2008 Olympic Games, the government can be at ease allowing athletes from all over the world to tread on this piece of blood-stained soil and participate in the Olympics?"

"China is making 'progress.' He is like a newly awakened giant, rushing forward in huge strides. The floor shakes because of his footsteps. Yet, how many people know that this giant is rushing forward with an extremely deep wound?" This was written by female Taiwanese writer Long Yingtai. Yes, over the past 18 years, China has witnessed dramatic changes in its economic, political and social arenas. The West has long since given up their sanctions against and isolation of China following June Fourth, and has resumed cooperation in the areas of the economy and trade, technology, culture and even the military. At present, Chinese leaders are making use of high-profile slogans such as "harmonious society" and "peaceful rise." Nevertheless, who can deny the fact that the disastrous aftermath of that brutal massacre, one of the greatest tragedies of our times, even after 18 years, is still unresolved. The wounds deep in the heart of the people are not yet healed. Because of this, the current political and societal landscape continues to deteriorate into disorder and imbalance. This proves that June Fourth, this bloody page in history, has yet to be turned, and remains a "knot" deep inside the people's heart.

Over these past 18 endless years, we, the victims of the crackdown, along with many persons of upstanding moral conscience, have made an effort using many different methods to return historical justice to "June Fourth." We have gradually come to understand from our blood, tears, and pain, that "June Fourth" is not only the misfortune of individual households, but also that of the whole nation. This misfortune originates from suspicion and hostility between individuals, from the Chinese people's indifference toward human life and values, and from a lack of civility and legal order in this land. However, the way to rectify this misfortune is not to counter violence with violence, nor is it for us to murder those of our own social class, as has often happened in Chinese history. One cannot rely on the present rulers' repeated slogans like the "three represents" or "people-friendly strategies." We can only rectify this misfortune by peacefully ending traditional authoritarian politics on Chinese soil and upholding the authority of modern democracy and constitutionalism.

Let each citizen cast away the submissive nature and historical inertia that have been passed down from the imperial era. Let each establish an understanding of the importance of universal human values. Based on this common understanding, we have abandoned the intolerant idea of "an eye for an eye" and the extreme position of countering evil with evil; we have decided instead to use the greatest sincerity and restraint as we seek to peacefully resolve the "June Fourth" heartache. For us, the victims' families, it is difficult and painful to make this rational decision. However, in order to avoid the escalation of conflict and the upheaval of society, we have done so.

We firmly believe history will prove that dialogue is the necessary route for justice and the reasonable settlement of the "June Fourth" problem; there are no alternatives. Nevertheless, history only offers limited opportunities for resolution, and to reject this present opportunity would be to continue this crime against the nation. Now is the time: those leaders who are truly open-minded and have the courage to fulfill their duties should wake up and make some kind of decision.

The world has entered the age of dialogue, yet mainland China remains behind, stagnant, in the age of resistance. This embarrassing and intolerable situation, which no one is willing to face, must end as soon as possible. We note that the Chinese government advocates the use of dialogue to solve differences and disputes in international affairs; we also note that the central government has already set a timetable for the direct election of Hong Kong's Chief Executive. We therefore have even stronger ground for our request that the government solve domestic differences and disputes through a similar method. If China, with its historical tradition of despotic rule, can strive to replace hostility with dialogue, it would benefit the entire nation and be a blessing to all people.

As this country enters into more dialogue, it will manifest more civility and legal order and less ignorance and despotism. We do not blindly believe in the idea of dialogue. It is difficult and tedious. But compared with resistance, dialogue is obviously the higher road. Dialogue should not lead society into opposition and hatred, but rather, into tolerance and reconciliation. In its past history and present reality, our country China has been enormously deficient in this kind of tolerance and reconciliation. Over the past millennium, including these last 100 years, our ancestors have suffered the side-effects of malignant interaction between the government and the people! Today, those with any amount of vision in China should step up their efforts and bravely make new strides forward to end the history of misfortune in our nation.

We are now living in a time of change from despotism to constitutional democracy. This is an unavoidable trend that is in accordance with popular sentiment. In this process of political change, the "June Fourth" incident has stood like a barrier that cannot be passed. The proper settlement of the "June Fourth" question would represent not only a conclusion, but also a new beginning. We hope wholeheartedly that all the representatives will, through your pragmatic endeavors, establish and strengthen the power of the lawmaking body so that settlement of the "June Fourth" issues can soon be added to the agenda. We sincerely hope for each of you that during this session of the NPC and the CPPCC, you do not go against your consciences or let your people down.

Finally, we also sincerely urge China's governing authorities to consider the situation as a whole. Grasp this golden, historic opportunity to respond positively to our aforementioned requests, and propose a timetable for dialogue on the "June Fourth" issues as soon as possible.

HRIC Olympics Take Action Campaign Individual Cases

[Submitted by Sharon Hom]

Case	Category	Detention+Sentence Date
Shi Tao	Journalist	11/24/04 Detained 4/27/05 Sentenced to 10 years
Chen Guangcheng.	Barefoot Lawyer	3/06 Detained 8/24/06 Sentenced to 4 years and 3 months
Mao Hengfeng	Petitioner/ Women's Rights.	6/30/06 Detained 1/12/06 Sentenced to 2½ years

HRIC Olympics Take Action Campaign Individual Cases—Continued

[Submitted by Sharon Hom]

Case	Category	Detention+Sentence Date
Hada	Mongolian Jour- nalist.	3/09/96 Detained 11/11/96 Sentenced to 15 years + 4 years deprivation of polit- ical rights
Yao Fuxin	Labor Activist	3/17/02 Detained 1/15/03 Sentenced to 7 years
Hu Shigen	June 4 Activist/ Writer.	12/16/94 Sentenced to 20 years + 5 years deprivation of polit- ical rights. Reduced to 18 years after 2 reductions.
Tenzin Delek Rinpoche.	Tibetan Religious Leader.	4/07/02 Detained 12/02/02 Sentenced to Death Penalty with 2-year reprieve 1/26/05 Sentence commuted to Life Imprisonment
Shuang Shuying	Evictions/Hous- ing Petitioner.	2/09/07 Detained 2/26/07 Sentenced to 2 years + fined 2,000 yuan
Guo Feixiong (Yang Maodong).	Lawyer/Editor	9/14/06 Detained 11/14/07 Sentenced to 5 years + fined 40,000 yuan
Huang Jinqiu (Qing Shuijun).	Cyber Dissident	9/13/03 Detained 9/27/04 Sentenced to 12 years + 4 years deprivation of political rights
Li Chang	Religion/Falun Gong.	7/20/99 Detained 12/29/99 Sentenced to 18 years + 5 years deprivation of polit- ical rights
Nurmemet Yasin	Uyghur Jour- nalist.	11/29/04 Detained 2/02/05 Sentenced to 10 years

CHINA LABOUR BULLETIN ARTICLE BY GEOFFREY CROTHALL AND HAN DONGFANG SUBMITTED BY ROBIN MUNRO (TO BE PUBLISHED IN THE FORTHCOMING BOOK "CHINA'S GREAT LEAP")

The slogan of the 2008 Beijing Games is "One World, One Dream." The Chinese word used for "One" in the original slogan is "tongyi," which means "the same." This word was chosen because it highlights the idea, as explained on the official Beijing Olympics website, that "the whole mankind lives in the same world and seeks the same dream and ideal." Yet this lofty message is at odds with the harsh conditions for the migrant workers who labored at the construction of the Olympic venues, often for the equivalent of five dollars per day. Han Dongfang was jailed for nearly two years for his participation in the 1989 Tiananmen democracy movement. In 1994, he founded China Labour Bulletin, a Hong Kong-based group that promotes labor rights and democratic trade unionism in mainland China. Geoffrey Crothall is the editor of China Labour Bulletin's English language website. He has reported on China since 1985.

On August 8, 2008, China will formally announce its emergence on the world stage as a powerful, prosperous and modern nation with a spectacular party attended by representatives from just about every nation on earth. For the Chinese government, the Olympic Games will be the culmination of nearly two decades of work stretching back to the original bid for the Games in the early 1990s. China's current leaders are determined that the political mission initiated by their predecessors, to make the Olympics both an international success and a source of pride for the Chinese nation, will be completed on time and without a hitch. By showcasing breathtaking new venues, Olympic medalists and Beijing's clean streets, the Games will doubtless be a success. But at what cost?

The all-consuming process of gaining, preparing for and hosting the Olympics has become highly politicized. Indeed, the government's mission to demonstrate its greatness through the Games could overshadow and distract from the increasingly serious social and economic problems Chinese workers have to contend with every day of their lives.

Some of these problems, such as the appalling health and safety record of Chinese construction sites, are right under the noses of Beijing's Olympic organizers. The construction workers who built the Olympic stadiums and support facilities, and completely overhauled Beijing's transport system in readiness for the Games, are almost exclusively migrant laborers who work in extremely hazardous conditions, usually have no labor contract, no work-related medical insurance, cannot form a trade union and have no right to collective bargaining.

OLYMPIC TORCH FAILS TO SHINE ON CONSTRUCTION SITES

In late July 2007, Sports Pictorial, a magazine published under the auspices of the Chinese Olympic Committee, interviewed a group of fifty-seven migrant workers on Beijing's Olympic construction sites about their work and living conditions. Most workers earned between forty yuan (about US$5) and sixty yuan a day, although a few earned more than eighty yuan. Many said they did not know how exactly they would be paid, and more than a third said they only got paid at the end of the year and received a small monthly allowance to live on. "I earn more than 1,000 yuan a month and get paid at the end of the year," said twenty-eight-year-old Hu Yaowu from Hebei "I've been married four years but can't afford to start a family."

Nearly all the interviewees worked ten-hour days, and only took days off if they were sick or had to go home to help with the harvest. They did not get weekends off, certainly no paid vacation, and most had no work contract or medical insurance. All those who suffered from minor injuries or illnesses at work paid for their own over-the-counter medicine or treatment at the local clinic. One worker, Liu Jiafu, who required surgery after incurring serious chest and leg injuries in a work-related accident, did have his medical expenses paid by his boss. However, when Liu, fifty-five, was released from the hospital, his boss had vanished and he received no compensation for his disability or loss of work. "Right now, I'm good for nothing," Liu told Sports Pictorial.

These problems are by no means confined to the construction industry. Lu Guorong lost her fingers while operating crude machinery at a small factory in a rural town on the Hebei-Shandong border, less than a day's drive from Beijing. Not only did the factory owner refuse to help her, he fired her two days after the accident because without her fingers she could no longer operate the machinery. Lu sought redress at the local labor bureau but in the arbitration hearing her official trade union representative appeared on behalf of the factory owner.

In the metallurgical industry, there has been a spate of accidents over the last few months. Thirty-two workers at a steel plant in Liaoning were killed in April

2007 when nearly thirty tons of molten steel poured onto the shop floor. And in August, fourteen mainly migrant workers died and fifty-nine were injured following an aluminum spill at a factory in Shandong.

Coal mining is probably still the most dangerous profession in China, and one of the most dangerous in the world. The number of accidents and fatalities has decreased from the horrendous highs of 2004 and 2005, when about 6,000 miners died each year, but there were still, according to official statistics, 1,066 accidents and 1,792 fatalities in the first half of 2007 alone. In August 2007, 181 miners died after two coal mines in Xintai, Shandong, flooded following torrential rains in mid-month. It is also important to note that the majority of accidents occur in small-scale illegal mines, precisely the kind of operations most likely to conceal accidents. The State Administration of Work Safety claimed on July 14 that it had uncovered forty-six coal mine accident cover-ups in the first half of the year, which suggests many others remain covered up and that the actual death toll is much higher than officially acknowledged.

In factories across China, workers are forced under threat of dismissal to labor in hazardous, even life-threatening conditions. In gemstone-processing factories where dust concentrations exceed permitted levels and visibility is down to one meter, workers must operate equipment without any form of silica dust protection; to complete order contracts, many workers in toy factories are forced to do overtime until they faint at their machines or even die from exhaustion. In these factories, bosses often illegally confiscate identification papers to prevent workers from quitting or running away when they can no longer endure the conditions, and many factories withhold most of workers' monthly wage packets, allowing them only pocket money.

FAIR PLAY FOR WORKERS?

These conditions are commonplace across China, but the government usually takes action when specific outrages are brought to public attention by an outside agency. When a report by Playfair in June 2007 exposed the use of child labor at factories producing official Olympic merchandise, the Beijing Organizing Committee of the Olympic Games revoked the license of one company and suspended three others. BOCOG's prompt response to the revelation of abusive labor practices at its licensee factories is a good first step, but it is little help to the workers if the government stops there. The workers are out of a job and have no guarantee that even if they find another job their work conditions will be any better. Instead of merely punishing employers caught in the act, the government should give workers the power to protect their own interests by granting them the fundamental freedoms to organize their own unions and the right to strike.

The response by the Beijing Organizing Committee of the Olympic Games to the Playfair exposé is very much in keeping with the government's heavy-handed approach to potentially embarrassing labor issues. On June 29, more than 3,000 workers at the giant Shuangma Cement Plant in Mianyang, Sichuan Province, went on strike to protest against the company's proposed severance package. Shuangma, a former state-owned enterprise, was in the process of restructuring after being acquired in May by the world's leading building materials company, Lafarge. Shuangma's proposed severance package of 1,380 yuan for each year of employment was the equivalent of the average monthly wage in Mianyang and included a clause which meant workers agreed to forgo all other retirement, medical and welfare benefits. When this package was presented to the workers on June 27 as the company's final offer, it was immediately rejected. Nevertheless, management went ahead and attended a planned banquet in Mianyang City with local government officials to celebrate their good fortune after the Lafarge buyout. They had just started the banquet when the strike began. Management and local government officials rushed back to the plant, but instead of addressing the strikers' demands, they sealed off the town, surrounded the plant with police and removed all Internet postings related to the dispute.

Likewise, when news emerged that the entire workforce of the Jinzhou bus company in Liaoning had gone on strike on July 19-bringing the town to a standstill-the authorities did not address the drivers' concerns over pay and privatization but merely blocked all news related to the strike. By contrast, the rescue of sixty-nine miners from a flooded coal mine in Henan in July 2007 was given extensive national coverage and portrayed in the official media as a miracle, without any analysis of how the miners became trapped in the first place. Blame for the accident was put on nature, rather than the human abuse of it. The August 2007 Xintai mine disaster killed 181 coal miners and was initially given much publicity, as authorities hoped it would provide them with another miraculous rescue story. However, as hopes faded for the trapped miners, we once again saw the usual media clampdown as families of the miners were ordered not to talk to the media. Those journalists who attempted to interview relatives were threatened with violence. After seven days, the government ordered a complete news blackout and all coverage in the official media of what had been a major news story ceased overnight.

ONE WORLD, ONE DREAM?

The intensification of news management in the run-up to the Olympics has been obvious to all; while foreign journalists have been told they will have unfettered access to all news stories in China during the run-up to the Games, domestic journalists have been warned not to report "false" (bad) stories, their movements have been restricted, and critical blogs and websites taken down. The television journalist who created the infamous "cardboard pork dumpling" story in Beijing, which claimed that vendors were selling dumplings made of pulped cardboard to unsuspecting customers, was jailed for one year and fined 1,000 yuan on August 12, 2007 for faking news reports and "infringing the reputation of commodities." Even the most innocuous criticism has been punished. At the end of July, two high school teachers on Hainan Island were given fifteen days administrative detention for posting bawdy song lyrics critical of local officials.

All this does not bode well for the Olympics. If, as seems very likely, these domestic controls are maintained, how will petitioners or protestors arriving in Beijing be treated? Will this traditional avenue for seeking redress be allowed any public expression at all in the capital next year? We have already seen an attempted march on Tiananmen Square on August 28, 2007, by 300 migrant workers demanding the payment of their rightful wages broken up by police before it could even begin. What will happen to the millions of migrant workers in Beijing who have no permanent residency? Will they be forced to return to their home towns? Will other social undesirables, beggars and mentally ill people be removed from the streets too?

It seems from the evidence so far that Beijing is more concerned with image management than dealing with the underlying causes of its problems. We believe, however, that the government should take precisely the opposite approach. Instead of trying to conceal the less flattering side of China in order to protect its own image, the government should grasp the opportunity presented by the international media spotlight to openly discuss the real problems facing the country. If the Chinese people and the global community could better understand these issues, everyone including the government would be in better position to resolve them.

CHILD LABOR IN THE SHADOWS

The specter of child labor, which BOCOG sought to exorcise so swiftly after the Playfair 2008 report, is an obvious example. Statistics related to child labor in China are designated "highly secret," and apart from occasional highly publicized crackdowns on employers the government has done little to address the problem. If, however, the use of child labor is brought out in the open and the government encourages the active involvement of all sectors of society in addressing the problem at its root, the greater the chances are that child labor can be checked and reduced in the future. Moreover, the government for its part should take urgent measures to reform the rural education system and provide sufficient funds to ensure that children stay in school, thereby cutting off the supply of child labor at its source. Many primary and middle schools in rural areas are currently funded almost entirely by fees charged to students' parents. And increasingly, these parents are deciding there is little point in them paying out thousands of yuan each year if there is little or no chance of their child going on to high school or university. As such, many children drop out in their second year of middle school (about age fourteen) and go straight to work, even though the legal minimum employment age in China is sixteen. The government could solve this problem by providing enough funding to ensure that the compulsory nine years of schooling in China are free and universally available. However, the government currently only spends about 3 percent of the gross domestic product on education, half the United Nations recommended minimum level of 6 percent.

In addition to the state's chronic underinvestment in education, public healthcare has declined to the point where millions of ordinary workers' families cannot afford to seek medical treatment or risk crippling debt if they do. In the past, workers' health care was covered by the state-owned enterprises. However, with the breakup of the state-owned enterprise system over the last decade or so, the healthcare system has broken down too. Many workers laid-off in the privatization process had limited or no healthcare benefits and were forced to seek work in the private sector where the intense competition for jobs meant that employers could very often set their own terms and conditions of employment. Moreover, the migrant workers who have now replaced state-run enterprise employees as the backbone of China's working class come predominantly from an agricultural background and have never had medical insurance, and are therefore less likely to demand it from their employers in the cities.

TILTING THE BALANCE OF POWER

Many employers ruthlessly exploit the passivity and stoicism of migrant workers, however many of those migrant workers are now beginning to stand up for their rights and demand not only appropriate wages but decent working conditions and proper health care. China's labor legislation, especially the newly promulgated Labor Contract Law, which gives individual workers a wide range of rights and safeguards, should in theory provide workers with adequate protection from exploitation and abuse. However, as has been demonstrated time and again since the enactment of the Labor Law in 1994, the Chinese government has routinely failed to enforce its own legislation. All the power resides in the hands of the enterprise owners, who in collusion with corrupt government officials (often part-owners themselves) can dictate how hard and for how long their employees have to work and for what reward. In some extreme cases, such as the 2007 Shanxi brick factory scandal in which thousands of workers were forced or abducted into slavery, that reward was imprisonment and physical abuse.

Not only can the government not enforce national labor laws, it can not even enforce labor related regulations and directives issued by the country's most senior leaders. In 2003, Prime Minister Wen Jiabao made it his personal mission to resolve the endemic problem of wage arrears in China; however, four years later, migrant workers, school teachers and factory workers across the country are still only receiving a small proportion of their promised salary. Again, following the spate of coal-mining disasters in 2004 and 2005, the prime minister spearheaded a campaign to improve mine safety. While visiting the families of victims of the Chenjiashan Coal Mine disaster of November 2004 in which 166 miners died, Wen Jiabao stated, "We must improve safety in the workplace. We cannot let another tragedy like this happen again. We must take responsibility for our miners." However the economic demand for coal in China combined with local level corruption in the coal fields has meant that production routinely exceeds safe capacity, and thousands of miners continue to die each year.

Given the government's persistent failure to enforce its own laws and regulations, the Chinese government should not merely draft more legislation to plug the gaps but empower the workers to defend their own rights. If workers had the right to organize their own grassroots democratic trade unions and the legal right to strike if necessary, they could literally play a life-saving role in ensuring coal-mine safety. Workers could demand that employers pay collectively negotiated wages in full and on time. Moreover, unions could act as an important facilitator bridging the gap between workers and management so that many of the violent protests that have erupted all over China in the last decade could be resolved or at least addressed through negotiation before protest became imperative. However, despite its commitment to "putting people first" and creating a "harmonious society," the Chinese government shows little sign of granting its citizens the rights or the ability to protect themselves. Rather we have seen a disturbing trend in which workers (like miners trapped in flooded coal mines) are portrayed as weak, pitiable and in need of rescue. And of course in this scenario, the only body that can rescue them is the government.

FLEETING GLORY FOR A FEW

Chinese workers are dying every single day in China, from industrial accidents and work-related illness. Most cannot afford decent medical treatment and have to suffer further from breathing polluted air, drinking polluted water and eating contaminated food. While the supreme health and fitness of the elite will be celebrated during the Olympics, the overall health of the nation is not advancing.

There are state-of-the-art sporting facilities all over China-private gyms, swimming pools, tennis courts and golf courses-but only the very rich can make use of them. The majority of Chinese citizens have limited or no access to such facilities. If the massive sums of money spent over the last two decades on bringing the Olympics to China had been spent on education, health care and sporting facilities accessible to everyone, Chinese people would be in a better position to actually enjoy the Games. And though the money has already been spent, there is still a chance that the international exposure brought by the Olympics will have a positive effect on workers' rights, which would indeed provide some lasting benefit to the country as a whole.

The opening date of the Olympics on the eighth day of the eight month of the eighth year should signify good fortune for the people of China as a whole and not just the privileged few. Thus far, however, the Olympics have failed to inspire even those ordinary workers closest to the project. Indeed, for many migrant workers interviewed at the city's Olympic construction sites, their contribution to China's Olympic dream is just another job.

"We don't need to know what these buildings are for. As long as we do the work and get paid, that's fine," a nineteen-year-old migrant worker named Dai told the Sports Pictorial. One quarter of the migrant workers interviewed by Sports Pictorial said they did not know exactly what they were working on and less than a third could correctly identify the opening date of the Games. The majority of interviewees had no interest in the opening ceremony or who would light the Olympic torch. Eight workers thought President Hu Jintao would light the torch, others nominated themselves, their work mates or famous movie stars such as Chow Yun-Fat. Many workers had no idea if they would still be in Beijing during the Olympics, most said they would go wherever the work was. For those who were confident they would still be in the capital, most did not think they would ever be able to enter the facilities they had built. "Attending the Olympics? That is for rich people! We can watch it on television, we can't expect any more than that," said thirty-year-old Zhu Wanming from Sichuan.

Zhu Wanming and hundreds of millions like him will be faced with great hardships for a long time after the Olympic closing ceremony, and it is the Chinese government's responsibility not only to ease those hardships but to give ordinary workers the power and the right and the ability to improve their own lives.

RESPONSES BY ROBIN MUNRO TO QUESTIONS FROM REPRESENTATIVE CHRISTOPHER SMITH

Question 1. Unfair labor is against our law. I hope that maybe this commission could pressure the USTR to take that up anew. Maybe your comments on that would be helpful.

Answer. As I stated in my written testimony for this hearing, "In addition, both multinationals and consumers in the West need to recognize that, in order to really achieve better and more acceptable labor standards for ordinary working people in China, the cost of China's exported goods will inevitably have to rise. Increased productive efficiency can only go so far toward providing the funds needed to provide Chinese workers with acceptable pay, reasonable working hours, mandatory work-related insurance coverage and safe factory conditions. The real problem is that these goods are much too cheap—and under-priced Chinese goods in Western shopping malls means continued labor rights violations in China.

"Both citizens and governments in the West should recognize, moreover, that higher labor standards for Chinese workers will also directly benefit the workforces in their own countries. By making it possible for Chinese workers to enjoy minimum acceptable standards, Western citizens and consumers will find that their own jobs become more secure, the trend toward casualization and part-timing of labor will reduce, and working-class families in many countries will benefit as a result."

For the above reasons, I think the AFL-CIO's submission to the USTR was well-founded and should have been acted on by the administration. Lack of labor rights in China clearly does, from the point of view of U.S. workers and those from other countries that import goods from China, amount to unfair competition. This directly disadvantages workers in the West, while at the same time preventing Chinese workers from achieving acceptable labor standards. In short, it's a lose-lose situation for workers everywhere.

Question 2. The venues for the Olympics. Have any of them been made with gulag labor?

Answer. To my knowledge, there is no evidence that prison labor has been used in the construction of the Beijing Olympic venues. However, it is well-documented that many prisons in China operate quarries and factories that produce raw materials for use in the construction industry, including stone and quartz goods and also cement, produced by prisoners and "reeducation through labor" camp inmates. For more information on this topic, I refer the CECC panel to a report I researched and wrote for Human Rights Watch in 1995, titled "The Three Gorges Dam in China: Forced Resettlement, Suppression of Dissent and Labor Rights Concerns" (*http://www.hrw.org/summaries/s.china952.html*). Appendix IV of the report contains a list of several dozen prisons and labor camps known to be directly involved, at that time, in producing raw materials for China's construction industry.

Question 3. Harry Wu has testified many times about how forced labor is endemic. But are any of the venues made by gulag labor? If not that, those who did work on the stadiums and the track and field aspects of it, what were they paid? What was the situation there? I think it is a very valid question.

Answer. As I said above, to my knowledge there's no evidence that prison labor has been used in the Olympic construction sites. As to how much the workers at these sites were paid, and what the working conditions were like: Nearly all construction workers in China are migrant workers from the countryside, and they typically work in dangerous working environments and are not provided by their employers with work-related insurance coverage, although that is mandatory for all workers under the Chinese labor law. Serious workplace accidents are common among construction workers, and it tends to be a lottery as to how much compensation—if any—they or (in fatal cases) their families are paid. Some employers pay a reasonable amount, but most try to pay out as little as possible, and they especially don't want to be saddled with the medical bills for workers injured on their sites. Also, construction workers in China typically have to work very long hours, often way in excess of the legal maximum working hours, and they often don't get paid once they've finished the job. Employers often try to withhold all or part of the wages, and workers then have to go to great lengths and expense—via the labor arbitration disputes system or via the courts—to get their wages paid. Since the official claims process is so onerous, many construction workers simply give up and never get paid.

Question 4. You might want to touch on the issue, if you could, briefly, of the missing girls in China. I said it at the opening. Very often, the human rights community has been mum on the fact that the family has been violated with impunity. Women have been raped by the state. Forced abortion is rape. It is horrible. It is used with particular impunity against the Uighurs, against the Tibetans, and against girls.

The Chinese government loves to say they have this policy or that policy. Since 1998 or 1999, they've been saying we signed the International Covenant for Civil and Political Rights, usually when one of their heads of state are heading to our shores, so that it allays concerns, just like the resumption of the human rights dialogue.

Answer. I have nothing particular to add on this issue, except to say that the government's coercive application of the one-child policy, and especially the use of forced abortion, is indeed a serious human rights issue in China. When the blind lawyer Chen Guangchen tried, a couple of years ago, to expose the widespread use of forced abortions in his rural hometown area in Shandong Province, he was arrested and sent to prison for over four years on trumped-up charges ("damaging property and organizing a mob to disturb traffic"). The government should have awarded him a prize for his civic-minded activities, but instead they persecuted him like this. That speaks volumes, I think, about the government's mindset on this issue.

○